Tales from These Old Bones

by

Patti Giglio

Copyright 2019 Patricia Giglio
All rights reserved

Cover Image: Mt. Albion Cemetery
Photo Credit: Heather Songin
Title Page Design: Andre Stewart

ISBN 978-0-578-59572-6

Notice: The information in the book is true and complete to the best of my knowledge. It is offered without guarantee on the part of the author. The author disclaims all liability in connection with the use of this book.

All rights reserved. No part of this book may be reproduced or transmitted in any form whatsoever without prior written permission from the author except in the case of brief quotations embodied in critical articles and reviews.

This book is dedicated to my husband Steve, who has shown me incredible support and love through the craziness of writing this book. My children, Liesl and Karl, who tolerate listening to my exciting "mom history lessons." And all my friends and family who encourage me to be who I am.

Table of Contents

Allegany County Poorhouse	1
Big Tree Inn	6
Catlin Hill	9
Clifton Spring Sanitarium	11
Cunningham Carriage Factory Brick-Throwing Ghost	16
Gang of Ghosts	23
Ghost on the Carter	25
Ghosts in the Stacks	27
Glass Works Ghost	28
Goodleberg Cemetery	37
Lake Monsters	40
Lily Dale	48
Newark State School	53
Rathbone's Ghost	57
Rochester Fata Morgana	59
Tavern on the Hill	63
The Cobblestone Inn	65
The Ghost of Glenwood Cemetery	68
The Ghost of Horseshoe Lake	70
The Jockey's Ghost	73
The Peddler	76
The Screamer of Glen Haven	82
Van Horn Mansion	85
Wayne County Jail	89
Wild Man of Steuben County	93
Witches of New York	96
Youngstown's Ghost	99

Allegany County Poorhouse

The original county poorhouse was built in 1823, a year prior to the passing of a law on November 27, 1824 regarding the establishment of county poorhouses across New York State. The state legislature voted to require each county in the state to build and maintain a county home for their residents that could not care for themselves. Those residents that were to be confined to or eligible for care at the poorhouse were *"habitual drunkards, lunatics (one who by disease, grief or accident lost the use of reason or from old age, sickness or weakness was so weak of mind as to be uncapable of governing or managing their affairs), paupers (a person with no means of income), state paupers (one who is blind, lame, old or disabled with no income source) or a vagrant."* The poorhouse was not only thought to be an institution to care for those unable to fiscally care for themselves, but also a forum to rehabilitate residents that had habits and characteristics that were less than favorable. One of the main goals was to turn uneducated and unemployed residents into productive members of the community. Lofty goals that were often not met.

When the poorhouse first opened men, women and children were cared for under the same roof, no matter what their ailments, mental deficiencies or deviant tendencies were. The children became easy targets of torture and abuse by other children, the criminally insane and sexual predators. In 1876, in order to protect the most vulnerable, the state required that all children living in the poorhouses across New York State be placed in orphanages or foster homes.

The county and state offices which oversaw the poorhouses were often corrupt and most facilities were found to keep their 2residents in deplorable conditions according to an 1857 report. It was said specifically of the poorhouse in Allegany County that "They were treated barbarously," Further in an 1864 report by Dr, Norton, the county doctor, the residents were kept in rooms or cells with straw mattresses on the floor, some having vermin sharing their living space with "no provisions for health or hygiene." Because of the various reports, community watch groups made regular visits to the county homes. The visits were usually scheduled or announced, so the overseers would put "a show" on for them. As the saying goes, they put lipstick on the pig, trying to cover-up what really went on behind closed doors.

In the July 28, 1880 issue of the Friendship Chronicle, the author describes their visit to the Allegany County Poorhouse. While the visit seemed pleasant enough, the encounters with the residents were interesting to say the least. *"A tall, thin old man was trotting backwards and forwards in one corner of the yard, indulging in a sort of go-as-you-please with himself. He had a rope tied about his waist and appeared to be well pleased with his occupation. This was David Crossman aged about 70, who passed some 30 years of that time in this place...Across the yard we are shown the Block House, filled with strong cells formerly used for refractory (unmanageable) inmates but now occupied by some of the most helpless cases. In one of these cells sat a very old colored woman. Our guide informed us that her name was Debbie Nelson; she came from Birdsall, was formerly a slave, had been in the House for over 30 years, and was certainly nearly if not quite 120 years of age. She occasionally walks into the yard but is quite blind."* The party left their visit at the poorhouse with this thought in mind, *"for even the grotesque oddities of some of the inmates could not drive away the remembrance of their lowly condition or the utter helplessness of life to the majority."*

As of the printing of the printing of the December 21, 1882

issue of the Buffalo Weekly Express, the Allegany County Poorhouse was one of the oldest, if not the oldest such institution in the state. It showed its age, in a state of severe disrepair, an awkward combination of wood and stone. According to the article, "…It has been necessary to prop one of the stone gables to prevent it from falling and the roof is worn and leaks badly." Also, right before the publication of the article, the building had been condemned – deemed unfit for human habitation. This was not news to those running the poorhouse, nor to the county, because in 1880 the county board of supervisors also deemed it "unfit for occupancy." No effort at the time, however, was made to repair or replace it. "The risk of fire throughout the buildings is imminent and such an event would, it is thought, inevitably entail great loss of life among the helpless, infirm and aged inmates." Construction finally began in 1883 to replace the dilapidated and unsafe buildings on the property.

The Allegany County Poorhouse as it sits today.

That imminent event happened on March 15, 1923 when the county poorhouse erupted in flames in what was referred to as the most horrible event in Allegany County history. Many papers carried the heartbreaking story as frontpage news in their morning editions, including the Olean Times Herald. The fire happened around midnight after an explosion in the basement, which killed Fred Scheu the poorhouse fireman instantly, rocked the building. At the time of the fire, the women's dormitory had twenty-three inmates living there; of which seven were bed-ridden, two babies under the age of one and fourteen others. The superintendent, William Hall and his wife rushed into the burning building and dragged some of the women out of the inferno one by one. Charles Sanborn, who oversaw the stables at the poorhouse, carried three women out of the building. When he went in to rescue a fourth, Sanborn was overcome by smoke and flames. He died a hero. All but the women who were confined to their beds were able to escape. The final death toll was nine. The women who were rescued received severe burns that they would recover from, but the nightmare of being surrounded by flames never went away.

For the people who rushed to the scene, their hands were tied. There was no aid that they could give as they listened to the screams for help that came from inside the burning building. The administration building, women's dormitory and the small building connecting them were destroyed within thirty minutes. The firemen couldn't put out the fire because the pump and tanks for the well that supplied the poorhouse water were destroyed when the boiler in the basement exploded, which was discovered to be the cause of the fire. A year after the fire, the buildings were rebuilt, and the facility remained open well into the 1960s.

The remains of everyone who perished in the fire were recovered and laid to rest. Initially the fate of Fred Scheu was unknown. Many thought that he had fled the fire to save himself, leaving the women in the building to be condemned to death. That theory was debunked on March 18th when his remains were discovered, his were the last of the remains to be found. The Olean Times Herald reported that "his skull was found intact. This was recognized from its peculiar shaped jaw and the number of gold teeth in it. Other bones were found in the same spot where the skull was."

Some of the remains of the fire victims were claimed by their family but the others, like some many that died at the poorhouse, were given a pauper's burial. The Until the Day Dawn Cemetery on Route 16 in Angelica has the unmarked graves of some of the county home residents. According to the Olean Times Herald, "These absolute paupers of society are buried directly behind and practically touching the only mausoleum in the cemetery and it is that of the most wealthy and prominent families in our county's history." There is also a cemetery on the grounds of the poorhouse. Each grave is marked with a simple metal marker with just a number, but no name to identify the deceased.

Rumors, of course, surround the abandoned buildings and the Allegany County Poorhouse has gained reputation of being haunted, and the present condition of the property does little to dispel those claims. Visitors who have found themselves inside say that there is a strong sense of a presence, though unseen, watching them. Pianos in the music room begin to play by invisible hands. The furniture and other objects throughout the buildings tend to move on their own and doors slam shut. It is as if life goes on from beyond the grave in the halls of the old poorhouse.

Big Tree Inn

The area surrounding the Genesee River Valley in what is now Livingston County was called Big Tree by the local Seneca Indian tribes because of the large oak trees that grew near the water. It was often used as a meeting place by both the Native Americans and settlers. In fact, it was the site of the signing of the Treaty of Big Tree in 1797, which ultimately removed the Indians from their tribal lands and placed them on reservations. Of the "big trees," there was one white oak that had a trunk almost 27 feet around. The massive tree stood there recording history for centuries until a flood brought it down in 1857. A section of it remains and is on display at the Livingston County Museum in Geneseo.

A simple log cabin belonging to Seneca chief Goondahgowah stood on a piece of land at Big Tree before it burned down around 1793. Forty-three years later Allen Ayrault and his wife Bethia bought the same piece of land to build their home on, which they called the Big Tree Lodge. The Ayraults were well-liked and respected in the community as Mr. Ayrault was a banker and the president of the Livingston County Bank. When Allen Ayrault died on February 4, 1861, Bethia remained in the house with her niece until she followed her husband into death twenty-four years later on January 6, 1885. The couple had no children, so the Ayrault's belongings were auctioned off and their beautiful home was put up for sale.

James W. Wadsworth had his eyes on the Ayrault's Big Tree Lodge and when the American Hotel burned down shortly after Bethia's death, he saw the perfect business opportunity. Wadsworth bought the building and hired William Nash, who was formerly in charge of the Osborne House and Powers Hotel, both in Rochester, to help oversee the massive renovations. The Big Tree Inn opened on September 13, 1886 as a luxury hotel and restaurant. Within two months Wadsworth sold the property to Nash for a healthy profit. It quickly became a popular destination with the finest of everything, and hosted notable guests like Theodore Roosevelt, Jean Harlowe and Arthur Brisbane. In 1902 Charles Baeder took possession of the inn.

The beautiful inn that the Ayraults built on Main Street in Geneseo in the early 1800s. Today it is a popular destination restaurant.

Baeder was a successful businessman with a favorable reputation that proceeded him. With the Big Tree Inn making a profit, he decided to expand his holdings. According to a 1915 piece in the Livingston Republican, Baeder bought the home of Judge WP Letchworth in Portage with plans to enlarge and renovate it as an in which he would call the Glen Iris, today it remains open. For some reason he sold the Big Tree Inn in 1923, only to buy it back six years later. He must have had an attachment to the inn that drew him back. When Baeder died on August 13, 1945, his funeral service was held there.

After his death, the Big Tree Inn changed hands several times. Eventually it became vacant and was an eyesore on Main Street. It had been foreclosed on in 1987 and needed major repairs, one of which was a large hole in the roof above the kitchen. The inn had a date with the wrecking ball, coming down to make way for something "shiny and new," but in a last minute move the State University of Geneseo saved it. The school made the necessary repairs and used it for student housing as well as accommodations for special guests. It changed hands one more time in 1992. Since then Davis Wayne has owned and operated the Big Tree Inn, offering fine dining and beautiful rooms for rent.

With a history spanning three centuries, it is no wonder that there is an energy that remains from those connected with its past. Bethia roams the halls of the Big Tree Inn and is often witnessed sitting near the window in her old room. The groundskeeper walks the property at night with his glowing lantern still making his rounds. And Charles Baeder makes his presence known in his own way. Some believe that there are guests of the old inn that have yet to check out. There has been a little girl in a green dress, as well as a man in a suit and top hat have been seen occasionally in the hotel.

Catlin Hill

All around the world there are stories of the ground being cursed, circles in the forest or field where no trees or vegetation will grow; like the famous Hoia Baciu Forest in Romania, the Devil's Tramping Ground in Bear Creek, North Carolina, and...Catlin Hill near Watkins Glen. Each of them have their own stories of ghosts and unexplained phenomenon that been passed down through the generations.

As we all know the oldest member of our community are experts at spinning a yarn. It is particularly true of the old timers in New York's Southern Tier region. They often told of a circle deep in the forest where not even a blade of grass would grow and how the ghosts and witches of Catlin Hill danced around it. In January 1938, the Democrat and Chronicle published an article retelling the story of a young man's terrifying encounter with one of Catlin Hill's spirits.

A Corning young man returned home yesterday on Falls Brook Train No. 3 after a few days visit on Catlin Hill. His appearance was decidedly woebegone, and he had the most harrowing tale to relate. It seems that the charms of a fair damsel attracted him to that vicinity, and last Friday he went Catlin-ward awooing. He expected to stay over Sunday, and he did too, but it was only through monumental nerve that he did it.

Friday night, so he positively declares, a white substance, resembling a woman of undoubtedly a ghost appeared in his room, her arms waving to and fro and beckoning him on. After a while the ghost disappeared, and he finally fell asleep. He told the family about his experience the next morning and somebody suggested that he had been drinking, where at he felt hurt. Saturday night he passed through the same experience only to be laughed at again when he related his second experience.

Sunday night came the climax. The ghost instead of disappearing after a while came toward the bed and crept in it. Frightened nearly to death, the Corningite jumped up. Huddled on his clothing and started out of the house on a mad run. All that night he dashed over Catlin Hill through fields and forest, with the ghost after him all the while. Until the dawn the ghost gave up the chase.

Wearied and frightened, the Corningite finally found his way to Watkins and thence home. He is now recuperating.

Clifton Spring Sanitarium

The Seneca Indians, as well as the other local tribes, had long been in tune with nature surrounding them and its medicinal powers, be it plants, herbs or even water. A spring ran through Clifton Springs for as long as can be remembered. The Indians believed that the pungent sulphur water that flowed from the spring held special curative powers. Early settlers who came to the area also discovered the powers of the spring, but until the Indians, they came up with a way to capitalize from it. In 1825, the residents of Clifton Springs built a bath house near the spring's main source, attracting people from as far away as Geneva and Canandaigua. They came to soak in the waters of the spring and fill their jugs with the spring water to use at home. (Life in the Finger Lakes, Summer 2002, "Coming Full Circle – the Clifton Springs Sanitarium")

Dr. Henry Foster developed a plan to utilize the powerful water, advertising a facility that channeled the medicinal qualities in order to benefit mankind. When he first harnessed the sulphur water for his water cure, a long line of patients waited for its opening on September 13, 1850. Business was booming and a larger building was soon needed. From 1856 to 1871 a major expansion was undertaken, forming the Clifton Springs Sanitarium Company. The ever-growing popularity of the sanitarium called for a modernization of the facility and additional services. The western half of the building was demolished in 1882 to make way for the much-needed renovations. When construction was completed, the sanitarium had become a 244-foot long, 91,500 square foot, five story brick building with a full-length veranda along the front. Inside the sanitarium, a beautiful stained-glass mosaic of the Last Supper designed by Louis Comfort Tiffany was installed in the chapel.

The services offered at the Clifton Spring Sanitarium was a blend of holistic and conventional medicine. Dr. Foster believed early on that the combination of the sulphur water and strong religious beliefs could restore the health and lives of many. He made it a practice of not just treating the body, but the mind as well. An article in Life in the Finger Lakes explained Foster's philosophy as the "mind and body were one, in health, illness and healing." It went on to say that "he always mentioned the soul first and the body second. He has out the two together, but always towering above the interests of the body are the interests of the soul…even when we are searching for physical health." A quote in the application for the National Register of Historical Places (on which it was placed in 1979) further describes the philosophy of the sanitarium. "Based upon curious mixture of current trends in 19th century medicine Foster's institution combines a water cure, allopathic (treatment of disease by conventional means) and homeopathic medicine with an insistence on the importance of spiritual health as part of all medical treatment. (preservationstudios.com)"

A 1909 postcard of the Clifton Springs Sanitarium. (source: author's private collection)

A 1906 advertisement for the Clifton Springs Sanitarium read – *"With fifty-five years' experience in the use of the best in medical, surgical, electrical and hydrotherapeutic treatments and the finest treatment rooms in the country, we can assure our patrons of the selection of that which will prove most helpful and suited for their individual needs...NO tubercular or insane cases received."*

The Clifton Springs Sanitarium was unlike any other around the region. As like most sanitariums and water cures; the importance of eating healthy, exercising and fresh air was promoted. But because it had a multi-faceted approach to treating patients, Dr. Foster and the facility played an important role in the ever-changing medical field. It became the first hospital in the region and second in the nation with capability to perform x-rays. The Occupational Therapy Association began at the sanitarium. Clifton Springs had the first open-ward psychiatric center in the nation. Dr. Foster was also a pioneer in hospital laboratory services that would be used in the study and diagnosis of diseases. He also set up one of the earliest nursing school which opened in 1892 and remained in operation until 1934. Added to the long list of accomplishments was the distinction of being the only hospital to have a chaplain and chapel on the property twenty-four hours a day, seven days a week – and always will. Dr. Foster's approach to medicine was revolutionary. He also thought it was important to fully involve the patient in their treatment, they should have a full understanding of their illness and what to expect on the path to recovery.

A brick chapel was built on the property and was dedicated on July 25, 1856. In 1926 the Woodbury Building that housed doctor and administrative offices was built on the campus which encompassed Sulphur Brook. After a century of declining popularity, the sulphur baths closed in the 1950s. A modern hospital was constructed in 1971 behind the sanitarium, and the original hospital building was converted into senior citizen housing.

Clifton Springs Sanitarium, the present building was completed in 1882.

Dr. Henry Foster died on January 15, 1901. His spirit has been seen in the lobby of the sanitarium as well as the Woodbury Building. Dr. Foster considered his work as a calling from God and he poured his life into the sanitarium, patients and community. It should not be a surprise that his spirit remained to watch over what he had created. When Dr. Foster retired in 1881, he and his wife turned over the operations of the Clifton Springs Sanitarium to a board of trustees with stipulations attached as to how it should be run. Perhaps he returns to make sure that his wishes are still being followed.

Hundreds of babies were born there, and thousands of lived were saved at the sanitarium over 165 years, but there were also many deaths that occurred within the walls. People claim to have seen shadow figures and mysterious appearing then disappearing bloodstains. Noises that could not be explained and slamming doors have been heard. Residents of the apartments in the original sanitarium building have reported disembodied voices and cold spots, as well as doors opening and closing on their own.

Cunningham Carriage Factory Brick Throwing Ghost

There was considerable excitement last night in the vicinity of that portion of the Cunningham Carriage Factory recently destroyed by fire. It was occasioned by the alleged appearance of nothing more or less than a ghost. A small boy minutely described the visitors from 'over there' to our reporter and the small boy evidently believed what he said. A number of citizens also saw the intruder, but Officer Fay, who went to the place purposely to view him, could not detect even the smell of brimstone. It is said that the officer did see a couple of bricks, which someone, ghost or otherwise, flung with a strong arm. The first appearance of the ghost was Thursday morning, when Cunningham and Sons' private watchman blew his whistle and screamed for the police. When Officer Crowley arrived, on a run, expecting to hear of a fire or burglary, he was solemnly assured that a ghost has thrown bricks at the watchman. Plenty of bricks were found, but the ghost had gone home. Tonight, there will no doubt be a crowd in waiting to see the ghostly brick thrower (Democrat and Chronicle March 28, 1880).

In the beginning, the Cunningham carriage factory encompassed almost an entire block between Canal and Litchfield Streets. It was one of the largest manufacturing complexes in the city at the time. They would later purchase all the houses on the west side if Litchfield Street to expand operations, and eventually all Peart and Hyland Alleys as well. The building not only houses the Cunningham Carriage Company, but also Charles E. Cunningham & Co., which made caskets. Death was the family business; you see the carriage factory specialized in horse-drawn hearses.

The first hearse they made was just before the Civil War. Early records show one of their first, if not THE first, was sold to a Pittsburgh funeral parlor for $2300, a small fortune.

During the New Orleans Cotton Exposition in 1884, the Cunningham Carriage Company unveiled a beautifully crafted and ornately designed "funeral car." What better place than Mew Orleans to debut one if the finest horse-drawn hearses, especially since the city is known for its funeral and Second Line parades. *"Although it was an extraordinarily beautiful vehicle for its time, the bold styling departure represented by this vehicle was considered by many of the undertakers* who viewed it as radical and too ostentatious for their use (coachbuilt.com)." Can you imagine something too flashy and ostentatious for New Orleans? No funeral parlor in the Big Easy wanted to buy the beautiful hearse, but a funeral home in Louisville, Kentucky snatched it up. Within two years, parlors all over the country wanted one.

The Black Moriah in Tombstone, Arizona was built in 1881 by the Cunningham company. It was one of eight made that year, and it is the only one that remains in existence.

An earlier model is in perhaps one of the most infamous towns in the United States. Inside the Bird Cage Theater Museum in Tombstone, Arizona, 'the town too tough die' and the site of the shootout at the OK Corral in 1881, is a hearse nicknamed the Black Moriah. The Black Moriah was built in 1881 by the Cunningham Bros Company in Rochester. Only eight were made that year and the Black Moriah is the last one in existence. It has 24k gold and sterling silver trim and was the first vehicle to be made with curved glass. From 1881 until 1917, the beautifully appointed hearse carried the remains of every citizen, except for six, to Boot Hill Cemetery for burial. Like the Cunningham factory itself, the Black Moriah had its own ghost stories. Visitors at the museum claim to see faces looking at them through the hearse's windows.

As for the fire that seemed to trigger the paranormal activity, or at least awaken it, on March 4, 1880 around 11 o'clock at night a violent electrical storm descended on Rochester. A powerful bolt of lightning struck the factory in which wood shavings and moldings were stored, igniting in a flash. The fire ultimately caused thousands of dollars in damages, displaced about forty workers and partially destroyed the building. Thankfully there were no casualties. However, there is nothing about the fire that offers an explanation as to the reason for the ghostly presence or why it insists on throwing bricks.

The natural curiosity engrained in human nature drove the Democrat and Chronicle to run a follow-up article the next day, March 29, 1880. The reporter for the newspaper tagged along with Officers Crowley and Fay, two Cunningham watchmen and another reporter on an investigation of the property. The men got more than they bargained for.

Yesterday morning the Democrat and Chronicle published under the heading 'An Eighth Ward Ghost,' brief particulars of some mysterious manifestations at night in the ruins of the recently burned Cunningham Casket Works on Canal and

Litchfield Street. The subject was treated lightly, because everybody who had heard of the inexplicable doings among the ruins was disposed to think that the 'thrown bricks' were only myths of the imagination. But Officers Crowley and Fay and other gentlemen who had visited the ruins and had bricks hurled at their heads with great force by unknown hands and from undiscoverable sources, were disposed to believe this if the missiles were thrown by human hands that the throwers were the sharpest, in preserving unbroken silence and in hiding in undiscoverable nooks, of any they had ever seen or heard about…About 7 o'clock in the evening the first brick was thrown at Watchman No. 2, Henry Wills, and he immediately fired his revolver in the direction from which he supposed it came from. But a careful search of every nook and crevice of the old 'spring shop' in which this occurred failed to discover so much as even a trace of the power that hurled the missile at the watchman – and this though the brick seemed to come from the immediate vicinity upon which his dark lantern shone. Of course, the report of the revolver had the effect to attract a larger crowd from without. But the watchmen had to continue their rounds of the long three-story carriage building running through from Canal to Litchfield Street, a distance of over 100 feet. Between the hours of 9 and 10 o'clock they had occasion to fire two more shots, but though every precaution in the way of dark lantern and careful listening was observed, they were unable to find the source of their trouble, which almost invariably came upon them just as they were passing from one large room to another and from the darkness of the room they entered.

About a quarter or half an hour after 11 o'clock Watchman Lark (Number 1), while peering into the darkness and listening intently for the slightest rustle or noise in the ruins, a piece of brick came like a dart from right in front of him and struck the lower part of the palm of his left hand, in which he held the dark lantern before his face. The brick came from exceeding force and cut quite a gash in Lark's hand. He held the revolver in his right hand and fired once. There was no sound as of anyone escaping, yet he searched the whole great room through and through without finding even a trace of the intruder.

...'Clang, Clang, Clang' sounded the first three strokes of the midnight hour as denoted from the adjacent church tower. Still they waited and watched without a word. Across the tops of the jagged upper walls remaining on the southeast part of the casket works the moonlight fell at an angle which reflected their outlines clear and black against the wall of the great north building which now contains the carriage factory. It was across the projecting upper edges of these long gaunt shadows, the Officer Crowley and the writer as they watched saw the black outlines of a human figure move. It seemed – as shadows always seem – rather to glide than to walk or run with an even tread. A glance at these jagged walls themselves showed nothing – yet there was the black and still moving shadow on the opposite wall.

...The writer and the two policemen went into the heart of the trouble – the old 'spring shop' – entering upon the ground floor. They were accompanied by Watchman Wills. The roundsman and the other reporter were out at the front of Canal Street listening. Down through a long room with cement floors and filled with rubbish the five men wended their way, lighted by only the straightforward streams of light from the lantern bullseyes. From this apartment they went into one where an old carriage had been mysteriously jostling up and down the night previous. Five minutes had elapsed, and the men had hunted. The reporter had both hands on a big wheel box and was shaking it. The watchman held the light with one hand and had the other on the box also. Both policemen stood in plain sight. Without a warning breath or rustle there came a 'bang!' and a piece of brick that had been thrown as if shot, fell from a pile of lumber back of the four men where it struck. Some of them *opened their mouths; all of them opened their eyes; each would have sworn that the brick came from a different direction than that claimed by the others.*

Both of the reporters left, leaving the watchmen and policemen to contend with the invisible brick-throwing entity. At around 4 o'clock in the morning, the newspaper received a call from Officers Crowley and Fay saying that since the reporters left three hours earlier, five more bricks were heaved at them. After a night of scouring the massive factory, they were no closer to discovering who or what as responsible for disturbing the neighborhood's peace.

Officer Fay was convinced that the bricks were not thrown by a ghost at all, but by Alexander Newville, another night watchman at the Cunningham carriage factory. The officer went as far as arresting Newville and hauled him off to jail. While in front of the judge, Mr. Cunningham came to the defense of his faithful watchman and the charges were dropped. The next day, March 30, 1880, the Democrat and Chronicle ran yet another follow-up story about the Canal Street ghost.

Jacob Lark, the other watchman, together with James Annett, testified that in one instance saw a brick pass in a horizontal line over the head of Newville, so that he could not have thrown it.

The publication and discussion of the peculiar manifestation on the Cunningham premises have set people talking. Many in the immediate neighborhood have become superstitious and frightened that they cannot sleep well at night, and, mention might be made of the name of one well-known lady living within a stone's throw of the carriage factory, who refused to retire to be or close her eyes at night.

Some of the facts have recalled to the memory of those who have resided in Rochester of the last forty years the facts that about thirty-five years ago a man named Schermerhorn owned and resided on the premises now bombarded by brickbats. There were then such unmistakable evidences that the place, whether the property could be sold for its value or only a fraction there of. They did leave, having sold out to James Cunningham, and there was no more trouble around the place – except, perhaps such as existed only in vague rumors or hallucinations. These, in and of themselves, were sufficient to frighten many woman and children to such an extent that for a long time Canal Street was a deserted thoroughfare at night. It may be added, however, that it has never been a street that enjoyed a great deal of travel or pedestrianism.

With the publication of the March 30th article, it became clear that whatever the beef was that the ghost had, probably had nothing to do with Cunningham at all. The spirit had been a long-time resident of the neighborhood.

Parts of the Cunningham carriage factory remain standing today. The building on the complex located at 33 Litchfield Street has been converted into 71 apartments with an authentic Cunningham carriage in the lobby.

One of the buildings on the Cunningham Carriage Factory campus. This photograph was taken near the dead end of Litchfield Street

Gang of Ghosts

The first, and largest, crime syndicate family in the 19th century was from New York, but not the five boroughs of the city. The Loomis Gang operated out of the small Oneida County town of Sangerfield along the Nine Mile Swamp. The matriarch and patriarch of the family taught their ten children how to lie, cheat and steal from their neighbors and hide the loot in the dense swamp. Their kids were fast learners and excelled in the family business, taking it to greater heights then their mother and father could ever imagine.

The Loomis Gang had particularly mastered the art of horse thievery. In fact, during the Civil War the cavalry of the Union Army was in desperate need of fresh horses. More than happy to serve their country in any way that they could, the gang stole horse from farms around the area and sold them to the United States government. That was just one type of crime in their repertoire. They also dabbled in extortion and dealing in counterfeit money.

For decades the Loomis Gang outsmarted the law. When they were arrested, through intimidation tactics and bribery, the charges would be dropped, and they would be released from jail. The gang wreaked havoc on the countryside and instilled fear in the minds of their neighbors, threatening severe and violent retribution if they retaliated.

By 1865, after nearly four decades of terror and menacing, the men of Sangerfield had had enough and they formed a posse to bring the family down. On Halloween night the vigilantes, secretly backed by the local police, descended on the Loomis farm and called Washington Loomis out. Washington had become the head of the family after his father passed in 1856.

As soon as he stepped out onto the back stoop, he was killed on the spot. Grove Loomis, another of the Loomis boys, was beaten, doused with kerosene and set on fire, though he did not die from his wounds. That night the Loomis homestead was burned to the ground, which brought the Loomis Gang's reign of terror to an end.

Or so it was thought.

On the anniversary of the raid on the Loomis farm, the sound of horse hooves can be heard beating along the trails winding through Nine Mile Swamp.

Bob Douglas was perhaps the only member of the Loomis Gang that criminal charges stuck to. Douglas was convicted of stealing a horse and sentenced by the magistrate to death by hanging, a common punishment at the time for the crime. The execution date was set for April 24, 1825. Before a crowd of hundreds of spectators, Douglas was placed in chain on top of his own coffin as he rode to the gallows in a wagon pulled by four black horses. The hooded hangman appeared on a coal black horse just before he pulled the lever that carried out the sentence of Bob Douglas. He was buried in an unmarked grave near Cameron Mills in Steuben County. Later the railroad laid tracks over top of his grave. Douglas's rest has been far from peaceful. According to legend, when violent thunderstorms roll through, the ghost of Bob Douglas is awoken from his eternal slumber. His spirit rides through the countryside as a black figure mounted on a dark horse.

Ghost on the Carter

As Captain Anderson slept in the cabin of his canal boat, a couple of men boarded, robbed and murdered him in the fall of 1899. A man's boat served as both home and office for much of year while plying up and down the Erie Canal trying to make a living, the boat became a part of him. Months after Anderson's murder, his canal boat was put up for sale and in the Spring of 1900, Lawrence Carter bought her. She was renamed the Carter. It would become evident that old Captain Anderson was tied to his boat in death as he had been in life. Even with a new owner in charge of her, his ghost stayed on.

June 1900, the Carter left her berth at a New York City dock and headed up the Hudson River for the first time under the command of Lawrence Carter. Her destination was the western end of the Erie Canal. When Captain Carter left on his maiden trip, he had a full crew, but by the time he reached Lockport only one crew member remained. Carter couldn't understand why one by one the crew abandoned ship, until the last man on board told an unbelievable tale.

His story was featured in the Buffalo Morning Express on August 8, 1900.

'One night,' said the canaler, 'when Grady was at the tiller, he suddenly let go of the thing and ran clear to the other end of the boat, hiding behind a big box. In a few minutes he woke me and the other fellow up and told us to come out on deck and see something. He was so badly scared that we thought he was crazy. But we went out on deck and looked aft, but saw nothing.'

'Oh, you wait a minute,' he said.

'We waited three or four minutes; then Grady shook all over.'

'Look at the tiller – see him?'

'I'm no believer in these superstitious things, but I did for a fact see something that night that worried me a little. A medium-sized man, with a night shirt curled around his legs and a slim, white beard that blew over to the side, stood at the tiller. That much was all right; nothing to be scared at. But when I saw two red blotches on his bald head and long streaks of blood running through his beard and along the front of his night shirt, I was a little bit creepy.'

'He came out of the cabin,' said Grady, 'and walked right toward me. Certainly, I ran; wouldn't you? It's a ghost, and a peach too, old man Anderson's. I heard about the murder.'

"We called the mule-driver and he looked at it. He almost died. I saw it myself, but I wasn't sure that I was all right because I had been drinking. It walked out of sight anyhow, and Grady took place at the tiler. He said he would quit the boat at the next stop, which was Lockport, and he did. And the rest did too.'

Word quickly spread all along the Eire Canal that the Carter was haunted. Sailors and boatmen were superstitious and a ghost on board was considered bad luck, even some would say it was a curse. This made it impossible for Mr. Carter to find a suitable crew to man his canal boat. After waiting a few extra days in Lockport hoping to hire on a few men, he could no longer delay the trip. He finally left with a load of grain for New York City with a crew of three – Carter's wife, his eighteen-year-old daughter, and Lawrence Carter himself. For as long as the Carter remained afloat, the sightings of Anderson's ghost continued.

Ghosts in the Stacks

The Jarvis Block in the historic town of Palmyra in Wayne County has a ghost, or should I say three and they all reside in the local bookstore. The brick building was built in 1876 after a devastating fire. Throughout the last fourteen decades, thousands of people passed through the doors of the hundreds of businesses. Some left their marks of history as they moved on while others never left. At any given time, footsteps can be heard walking on the second floor or around the bookstore itself. The spirit of a long dead merchant wanders the shop looking for his wife that died in a fire, refusing to cross over without her. Other times books fly off the shelf by an unruly ghost that doesn't approve of the arrangements the owner has made. But perhaps the most heartbreaking of all the spirits is that of a World War II soldier sent off to battle, leaving behind the love of his life. The young man dies far from home and his true love never marries. He waits in the bookstore for her to pass on to join him for eternity. His presence, filled with sadness and hope, is felt but never seen.

The Dog Ear Book on Main Street in Palmyra plays host to 3 spirits spanning 2 centuries.

Glass Works Ghost

Victorian America was fascinated with spirits and the paranormal in the late 19th and early 20th centuries, more so than today (if you can believe it). Rarely do you find an encounter with a ghost covered in a newspaper, it is an extra special find when it is subsequently followed up in three additional articles. The entire paranormal event that unfolded in Rochester's Nineteenth Ward in the Fall of 1910, had the community in a frenzy. I would like to share parts of the articles with some historical background added in between.

> Rochester Democrat and Chronicle, September 10, 1910
> *No use hurling rocks at ghosts – Glass works spook laughs at cobble stones – watchman flees from it*

The ghost of the glass works, the only authenticated spook in Rochester, was on the job last night and furnished food for reflection to half the residents of the lower end of the Nineteenth Ward, not to mention reporters and policemen, who are supposed to be coldly skeptical in such matters.

The disappearance of Millard Wiltsie, aged 32 and the father of four children, from his home at no. 417 Plymouth Avenue, renewed interest in the spirit that, tradition has it, has haunted the glass works in Plymouth Avenue, a short distance south of the railroad bridge, for half a century. Detective Andy Andrews was sent out to look for Wiltsie and was astonished to find that the former watchman of the glassworks as supposed to have fled from the ghost.

There was a crowd of residents of the neighborhood around the entrance of the glass works, last night, when a reporter got Watchman Herman Darling to let him go with him on his rounds.

"I don't know anything about a ghost," said Mr. Darling defiantly, as he trod his way, lantern in hand, through the eerie holes and corners of the glass works. "You needn't ask me about that. Besides, nobody ever saw this stuff before midnight or 1 or 2 o'clock."

The party of investigators had reached the shed in the rear of the glass works abutting on the Pennsylvania Railroad tracks, when Mr. Darling made these remarks. Just as he spoke a hazy moving-picture sort of figure appeared on top of the shed. It was an etherical kind of apparition, about as hard to describe as Hailey's Comet, but it was there, alright.

"See that?" inquired former policeman Jack Moran, who had been summoned by the neighbors to lay the ghosts.

"I see something and I'm going to see if it is solid," replied the reporter and he lightheartedly hurled a large, flinty rock at the apparition.

It was a good, true heave and should have dented the midriff of the ghost, but it went through him, or her, or it, or whatever a ghost is. That settled it. There's no use tearing up the streets to fling cobbles at people who have no insides, so the posse adjourned to the Plymouth Avenue entrance to the works, where the city has thoughtfully established lights and the lighted windows of the saloons on the other side of the avenue make one think of home and supper.

Has Uncanny Reputation

The northern section of the Nineteenth Ward is torn up over the question of the glass works ghost. The place had an uncanny reputation before the Reed Company, the present proprietors, ever saw it. Fifty years ago, it was the scene of a gruesome murder of a Jewish peddle by an Irishman and a negro and the old inhabitants of the ward whisper about with a shudder. About ten years ago a glassblower named Welch was found dead and, while the coroner could find only natural causes for his death, the neighbors stoutly assert their belief that he was killed by the ghost.

Tim Mahaney, a very well-known resident of the ward, who formerly held the responsible position of night watchman of the big factory, quit it because of the spiritual manifestations, it is currently reported. Wiltsie, who disappeared last Tuesday, was a sober, responsible man, and his elimination from home is accounted for by his family and friends only on the grounds of fear of the ghost. Two young sons of Wiltsie were at the gate of the glass works when the reporter made his rounds with the watchman last night...

Millard Wiltsie, the watchman who disappeared, had an unusually hard experience with the ghosts. He had worked in the place four years and had seen many creepy things, such as the apparition that the reporter tried to put a rock through last night, but he didn't mind that. The watchman carries a time clock and there are keys distributed about the plant, which is required at intervals, to get and insert in his clock. When Wiltsie was doing this, last Monday night, someone or something rapped him violently on the knuckles.

Two Ghosts One Too Many

The watchman stood this as long as he could, but when his lantern was extinguished by a breath of exquisitely icy air and he himself was flung on the floor, he ran for the street. Two neighbors who chanced to be passing naturally inquired what was the matter, and Wiltsie told them.

"Out on the shed there are two ghosts," he is said to have gasped. "This thing has been getting on my nerves for a long time and I can't stand for two ghosts."

The inference is that Wiltsie would have stood for one ghost, as being part of his job. Some friends of his said last night that he was probably on a visit to his brother in Watertown.

The glass works will be patrolled by policemen and citizens tonight in an effort to ascertain the character of the strange apparition. It was remarked in Columbia Avenue and even up as *far as Flint Street that it was strange that the ghost should walk on a Friday night, and it is thought the chances of getting him tonight are good. The members of the Reed firm, who own the plant, declined to talk for publication, but say the ghost talk is "all rot." Maybe it is but you can't tell anyone in the election district so. The Nineteenth Ward is not going to be deprived of its ghost if it can help it.*

The glass factory at 380 Plymouth Avenue was originally opened in 1862 as the Rochester Cooperative Glass Works by workers from the Clyde Glass Works, which has a ghostly connection of its own. Clyde Glass Works owner Charles Ely may be one of the spirits that haunt the Smith-Ely Mansion (aka Erie Mansion) in Clyde. At the time of the article's publication, the factory was known as the FE Reed Glass Company, owned by Frank E. Reed.

Part of the original article speaks of a gentleman named Welch that people believed was killed by the glass factory ghost. James Welch was a 35-year-old glass blower employed at the factory. On the morning of March 29, 1899, he died mysteriously near the Western New York and Pennsylvania Railroad tracks. His body was found half an hour after he left work. An autopsy performed on the body was unable to determine a definite cause of death.

Rochester Democrat and Chronicle, September 12, 1910
Ghost parties latest wrinkle – apparitions of glass works upsets vicinity – opinion divided on ghost – some Nineteenth Ward residents think picture machine man has been busy while others maintain belief in the ghost

Ghost parties were popular in the northern end of the Nineteenth Ward Saturday night and last night, as a result of the report of the apparition at the glass works in Plymouth Avenue. People who had social arrangements keeping them out until about midnight made it a point to troop over to the glass works in the hope of seeing something.

Aside from this public curiosity there was nothing in particular doing on the ghost last night. The gate of the factory was closed to visitors and the watchman made his rounds alone and undisturbed by spiritual manifestations. The former watchman, Millard Wiltsie, has not reported, and it is believed he is visiting his brother in Watertown and will not return to the works.

Opinion is divided as to the ghost. Some residents of the neighborhood think a joker with a stereopticon picture machine has been busy throwing weird vision on the heavy night air back of the glass works. On the other hand, there is the experience of Millard Wiltsie, who was manhandled by the ghost, it is said.

Society May Investigate

The Society for Psychical Research is expected to communicate with a local correspondent as to the phenomenon...

At the house of Hose 7, just south of the bridge, the firemen did not care to talk for publication, but some of their friends said that strange things had been reported there. It is said that people passing the glass works have been called to by a ghostly figure, which requested a chew of tobacco. These occurrences were inevitably after midnight.

Placard Quickly Destroyed

Saturday night a sign was pasted on the factory wall reading '$5,000 Reward for the Ghost. West Side Ghosts Association.' It was torn down as soon as the watchman's attention was called to it. Scores of well-dressed men and women lingered about Plymouth Avenue, in expectation of seeing something, until Patrolman Puffer came along and cleared the sidewalks.

Whatever the outcome of the investigation of the ghost it has been made an impression on the vicinity and ghost parties will be the proper thing this winter. Several have been planned for evenings this week, the participants to be robed in white and execute weird dance movements. These parties will walk past the glass works on their way home, just to see if there is 'anything doing on the ghost.'

Rochester Democrat and Chronicle, September 18, 1910
Oil habit had ghost on the run – Spook's antics explained by one who knows – Former watchman is here – Wiltsie insists he didn't quit because he couldn't stand for two ghosts and that he doesn't fear any ghost in neighborhood.

Millard Wiltsie, of no. 417 Plymouth Avenue, who was reported to have been scared away from his position of watchman at the glass works in Plymouth Avenue by two ghosts, visited the Democrat and Chronicle office last night and declared emphatically that there never was but one ghost and he wasn't afraid of that one.

'I wasn't scared away,' said Mr. Wiltsie. 'I quit because I wanted to and told the foreman I was going. The ghost never hit me on the knuckles and put out my lantern. That was another watchman. He went to the firehouse across the road to get his lantern lit and the firemen couldn't light it because it was empty. 'Mother O-Mike!' says he, 'the ghost drunk the oil out o' the lantern.'

'That's how that stuff started. I ain't afraid of anything on Plymouth Avenue, not Exchange Street either. There was a German watchman there, who followed the Irishman I was telling you about and he saw spooks right along, but they never scared me.'

'You did see something, though?' suggested a reporter.

'Well, I'll tell you. One night there was something white on the shed and it made a kind of noise, like a Scotch bagpipe with a bad cold, and I went right up on that shed after it and it jumped down onto the Pennsylvania Railroad tracks and beat it up the rails. Then there was another figure up the track and heard them laugh in a creepy sort o' tone, but I wasn't afraid. I'd just as soon take that job of watchman tonight.'

'You admit you did see something, though?' it was insisted instead.

'Why, sure I saw something. So did the other watchmen they had before me. What I am telling you is that I didn't run away from it and that there was only one of 'em on the shed. Say, who was the reporter that shied the brick at the ghost?'

'I'm the man,' responded the reporter, modestly.

'Did you hit him?' whispered Mr. Wiltsie, with unfeigned interest.

The reporter was compelled to confess that he didn't and the ex-guardian of the glass works was genuinely sorry.

'One more thing I'd like to know,' he said. 'Who was this kind of friend of mine that said that I was scared when I rushed up to him and told about two ghosts? I never was scared at all. I'll buy a couple of papers tomorrow if you'll tell me what that 'particular friend' of mine as that told that.'

...Mr. Wiltsie did not go to Plymouth Avenue last night, but the information he gave the Democrat and Chronicle was conveyed to the members of the Nineteenth Ward Improvement Club and they took action at once. At a meeting presided over by Bird E. Crahan sent here from the New York branch of the Society of Psychical Research, regardless of expense. Professor Crahan will endeavor to talk with the ghost and get him to transfer his field of operations to the Vacuum Oil Works in Exchange Street.

The story of the Glass Works Ghost was carried in newspapers across the country. As result, the newspaper, the glass works, and the Nineteenth Ward Improvement Club received offers of help. Some of the letters were from "creditable" people and organizations, while others were a little off the wall. After about a week after the news broke about the ghostly encounters, the Democrat and Chronicle got a letter in the mail from a Voodoo doctor offering his services. The final article in the glass works saga was quite comical for the reader, though I am sure that the author of the note was rather serious in his sentiments.

Democrat and Chronicle, September 21, 1910

Black cat bone or pilot snake – or graveyard sand, that spook may shake – guess what dope to take – voodoo doctor wants good job, the 19th ward of ghost to rob; asks expenses they'll produce, club is broke – what's the use?

There is a ghost hunter on the trail of the glass works spook and all he asked as renumeration for using his expert skill is 'a little sum of money and all his expenses paid.' A couple of letters, with a Cleveland date line, have been received at the Democrat and Chronicle from the spirit chaser and they bear internal evidence of his knowledge of the subject and incidentally, of his color and previous condition of servitude.

The first letter seems to have been dictated to the ghost hunter's assistant, who writes a better hand and spells more nearly according to Hoyle, though far from so interestingly as the original spook layer. Here it is in all its purity and strength:

'For Chairman Ghost Committee 19th Ward Rochester, NY. Deir Sir, I heard you had so' ghoses up there that you can't get away. I'm one who can take away any ghoas. I will take him away for a little sum of money and my expenses paid and guanatee the ghoas will never come back again. Not knowing you, but this is the Voodoo Doctor from te South. Dr. George I Walker, 2725 Central Ave., Cleveland, Ohio.'

The other letter strikes the ghost editor of the Democrat and Chronicle as being so convincing that it ought to result in an apparition by the Common Council to bring the ghost hunter here. It is addressed like the other one and runs:

'Ez uh administration uv what my first letter sayed. I kin take yah ghos away in diffunt ways. I kin use de black cat bone, de yaller sand fum a grave yahd, er I kin use snaix. All yoh hez to do is say wich. Ef it aint to much trubble jes tell me what kine uh talk dis ghoas uses, en I kin study out de easy way the gen in a good slam. I year ye got a rattek snaix man what kin cunjoor? I kin beat him wif a pilot snaix. Hopin to year dum you soon. Im *de Voodoo Doctor fun de souf.'*

There are so many ghost clubs in the Nineteenth Ward lately that the ghost editor was puzzled what to do with these epistles, but finally appealed to the treasurer of the Comet Club, an organization of gentlemen residing in the Rapids vicinity. The treasurer regretted that the organization had been financially dented by contribution to the Fourth of July celebration back of West High School, further embarrassed by betting that the airship would fly across the city and finally crippled by the defalcation of the president with the last of the funds, which the treasurer had incautiously lent him to bet on a ball game.

A committee was hunting for the president near the brickyards, said the treasurer, and, if they got him and shook anything out of his clothes they would send the ghost a hamper of luncheon, directions for riding the freights and a pass that would protect him against the Lake Shore Gang.

The Nineteenth Ward Improvement Club was appealed to in vain, the president profanely suggesting that the editor pay for the laying of his own ghosts. In the saloon in Plymouth Avenue they denied, with stony glares, that there had ever been a ghost and seemed sensitive over the beverages sold in the immediate vicinity of the glass works. So, there the matter rests. The Voodoo Doctor is respectfully informed that this particular ghost asked belated pedestrians for a chew of tobacco so he can prescribe the dope suited to that line of ghostly talk.

As the article states..."so there the matter rests." There were no further encounters recorded, nor reported in the newspaper. The FE Reed Glass Company is no longer in existence on Plymouth Avenue. However, maybe there is someone who once worked at the factory that might have had some otherworldly experiences and has details to share.

Goodleberg Cemetery

When I first visited the Goodleberg Cemetery, I felt a sense of calm and tranquility as soon as I stepped off the top step leading to the burial ground. It seemed, as my friend Heather also observed, that even the wind sounded different there. The rural cemetery is nestled in a valley surrounded by tree-covered hills south of East Aurora. Like most early burial grounds, it is small with fewer than 90 graves on its beautiful 1 ½ acre lot. The graves had been lovingly tended to until the last family member moved away or passed on themselves. For over a century, the Goodleberg Cemetery was virtually unknown, except to those hunting for their roots…that us until the rumors started. As a result, a great deal od damage has been done over the years to the grounds and headstones by people trying to see for themselves if the rumors of ghosts and red-eyed demons were true. The sanctity of the land had been disrespected again and again.

The origin of the hauntings goes back almost seventy years with the main story/rumor revolving around a local doctor named Albert Speaker, who lived about ½ miles from the cemetery. If even half of the rumors about Speaker are true, he was a terrible monster of a man bordering on serial killer. According to the legends, he had an office in him home, out of which he performed emergency operations and illegal abortions. The nature of the procedure was dangerous to the patient, and sometimes a mother lost her life alongside the fetus she was trying to rid herself of. When a death did occur, Dr. Speaker needed to dispose of the bodies discreetly. So, under the cloak of darkness he carried the bodies down the hill and dumped them into the pond behind Goodleberg Cemetery.

It is unknown how many young women and tiny babies were deposited in this watery mass grave. This, however, wasn't the only skeleton that Albert Speaker hid in his closet. He, supposedly, had an unnatural fascination with the reproductive organs of the female anatomy and had a morbid collection of then preserved in glass jars. Whether or not this is true will never be known. Mystery surrounded Dr. Speaker's death in October 1948. The official cause of death was listed as a heart attack, but many believe that Speaker was afraid that his disturbing past was catching up with him and he took his own life. Someone went to great lengths to make sure that whatever he worried about being found would never see the light of day, because on Halloween night Albert Speaker's house/office burned to the ground.

Aside from being connected to this abysmal man, there are other parts to the rumor that Goodleberg Cemetery is haunted. People have given eyewitness accounts of hell hounds lurking around the cemetery. Those who have heard "the howl of the dogs claim that the sound is terrifying and evil." Hell hounds are large black dogs with red or green glowing eyes that are believed to be evil harbingers of death. They are also traditionally known to be protectors of burial grounds, gathering lost souls and ushering them into the afterlife. Perhaps they are searching for the souls of the aborted babies and their mothers that had been discarded in the nearby pond.

Other supernatural occurrences people have experienced include hearing a newborn baby crying behind the cemetery. While others have seen the ghost of a country doctor walking along Goodleberg Road carrying a black medical bag...in broad daylight.

And what haunted cemetery doesn't have a story of a curse attached to it. If anything is removed or damaged at the cemetery, the person or persons responsible would experience bad luck, health issues, or unexplained injuries until everything is made right. Take heed to this warning that if you visit Goodleberg Cemetery, leave everything as you found it.

Goodleberg Cemetery, the final resting place for nearly 90 people including many veterans of American wars.

*If you choose to visit Goodleberg Cemetery, please leave no trace of your visit when you leave and respect the peace of these final resting places.

Lake Monsters

It seems that every lake has a story of a lake monster that lives in its watery depths. The most notable lake monster in New York State is Champ, who was first sighted in 1609 by Samuel De Champlain for whom the lake is named. However, those who live west of the Adirondacks and Catskill Mountains will tell you that "their lake monster" has Champ beat...hands down.

The Finger Lakes region has six large lakes as well as six smaller ones that were formed by receding glacial ice thousands of years ago. Three of the lakes; Cayuga, Seneca and Silver Lake boast claims of terrifying and unimaginable sea creatures that lurk beneath the glass-like surface.

Old Greeney is the lake monster that calls Cayuga Lake home. At 38 miles, Cayuga Lake is the longest of the Finger Lakes and it has a depth of 435 feet, which makes it one of the deepest lakes in North America; so, who knows what else lives in the darkness. The first reported sighting of Old Greeney was in 1828, and eyewitness accounts have been documented in local newspapers and lore for nearly two centuries since.

The Hornellsville Weekly Tribune told its readers about an encounter on August 13, 1886. *"The Cayuga Lake Sea Serpent has been heard from again; this time in the vicinity of Atwaters Landing...'We were several rods from the shore leisurely rowing about when we saw a large black object suddenly rise from the water to a height of several feet. The snake was some thirty rods to the north of us, but his head as it appeared above the water, seemed to be fully two feet broad, with large bright eyes.'"*

An article appeared in a September 1894 newspaper chronicling the following account. "*...Last Wednesday a well-known Ithaca gentleman as on the western shore of the lake having with him two hired men. Looking out into the lake he was astonished to see what appeared to be a man with a hat on his *head swimming around about three hundred feet from shore. The swimmer was apparently tireless for the men watched for fully half an hour. Then a pair of marine glasses was procured and looking through them what the gentlemen saw was not a man swimming but a large serpent, with its head high out of the water...why is it not within range of possibilities for such an animal to exist in the waters of such a large lake."* It became hard for a local newspaper to find men willing to cover stories in certain areas of the countryside, as told on January 5, 1897. *"The members of the journal staff have been living with daily anticipation of the monster's appearance and have actually shunned assignments which would take them near the water's edge for fear of being compelled to shudder and tremble at the sight of him."*

Apparently the course of the Old Greeney tale changed a little in the 1920s. People started to believe that there were two sea serpents living in Cayuga Lake instead of just one. Each was estimated to be twelve to fifteen feet long. People still reported personal encounters with the serpent, some of which turned violent. In 1974 Steven Griffin, a local teenager, claimed to have been attacked by Old Greeney. He said that he saw a large serpent while swimming in the lake. Before Griffin knew it, the creature grabbed his arm in its powerful jaws and broke it.

Two more sightings were reported after that. First in 1979, by a group of friends boating on the lake. The men cut the engine to avoid what they thought was a large log or tree in the water, just missing it. They couldn't believe their eyes when they saw what happened next. As it slowly slipped into the dark depths and disappeared, they found that it was not a log at all, but instead a thirty-five-foot serpent.

The final appearance, that is known to this author, came twenty years later and was relayed in a December 2009 newspaper article. *"I've been face to face with Old Greeney; not more than one hundred feet away from me as I stood on the northern shore of the lake, eight or nine years ago. It raised its triangular tooth filled jaws with aquatic plants hanging from its half-opened mouth to break the surface for only about three seconds before once again submerging..."*

Cayuga and Seneca Lakes are connected by a series of underground channels. A portion of the population believes that the serpent in both lakes are one and the same, traveling through the channels at their leisure.

The idea of a serpent living in the waters of Seneca Lake, which can reach depths of 618 feet, began in local Native American folklore. They believed that the lake had no bottom and that a "monster" lived in a lair deep within the blackness.

July 14, 1899 the Otetiani, a sidewheel steamboat, had a close encounter with the beast as they were returning to Geneva from Watkins Glen with a load of passengers. About fourteen miles from the Geneva dock, around Dresden, the boat came across something strange in the water. Frederick Rose, who was the pilot of the Otetiani, saw what appeared to be a capsized boat in front of them. As they got closer, Captain Herendeen had a small boat lowered to inspect what was in the water. Suddenly, the object began to move slowly away from the Otetiani, and the captain ordered them to give chase. The beast turned towards to steamboat and raised its head to bear two rows of razor-sharp teeth. Seeing that it was the infamous sea serpent, Herendeen ordered Rose to ram it with the bow of the boat in order to either capture it or tow the dead carcass to Geneva. *"Everyone was fixed on the monster and hardly a person was breathing normally. While the boat was yet some distance from it, the monster again looked at the boat, sank out of sight and the boat passed over the spot where it had been* (Ithaca.com)." The order was given to turn the boat and strike the creature with the paddlewheel. At full speed, they struck the sea monster with enough force to knock people off their feet and mortally injure the monster. *"It raised its head, gave what sounded like a gasp, and lay quiet. Its spinal column had been broken and it was dead."*

Lifeboats and men were deployed to tie ropes around the carcass so it could be towed to Geneva, but the beast was too big and heavy. Slowly it sank to the bottom of the lake. When the ship docked, the excited passengers and crew told the typical "fish tale," describing the creature as being anywhere between twenty-five and ninety feet long. Professor George R. Elwood would give the most credible testimony. He believed it to be a clidastes, a marine lizard that was thought to be extinct for over 66 million years.

Elwood described the creature as being around *"twenty-five feet long, with a tail which tapered until within about five feet of the end, when it broadened out and looked much like a whale. The creature weighed about one thousand pounds. Its head was perhaps four feet long and triangular. Its mouth was very long and armed with two rows of triangular white teeth as sharp as those of a shark, but in the shape more like those of a sperm whale. Its body was covered with a horny substance which was much like the carapace of a terrapin as anything else of which I know. This horny substance was brown in color and of a greenish tinge. The belly of the creature, which I saw after the rope slipped and the carcass was going down, was cream white. Its eyes were round like those of a fish, and it did not wink."*

A week after the 1899 incident, a Geneva Gazette reporter suggested that the passengers of the Otetiani stopped at several of the many wineries on Seneca Lake and were "prepared to see creatures and monsters of all shapes and sizes."

There have been at least 20 reported sightings of the Seneca Lake Monster since the July 1899 fatal incident with the Otetiani, giving credence to the theory that there may be a family of sea serpents instead of just one.

In August 1914, a couple out on the lake enjoying a romantic rowboat ride, witnessed the creature as its head broke the surface of the water. After taking his terrified date back to shore, the man returned to the water with a .38 revolver and a friend. When the lake monster surface again, the man shot it and the monster slipped back under water. Eighty years later, in 1995, a woman staying at a hotel in Geneva became very shaken after seeing a large serpent-like creature, only about 600 feet from shore, jump out of the water and immediately plunge back in.

Artist's rendition of the Seneca Lake Sea Serpent

The City of Geneva embraces the legend of the lake and on August 5, 2015 they passed historic legislation in regards to the lake monster residing in the water off their shore. Geneva Municipal Code Chapter 206, Section 2: Hunting or Trapping of Seneca Lake Monster Prohibited reads as follows – *"The hunting, trapping or cause of harm to the serpent termed the Seneca Lake Monster or any of its descendants is prohibited. No person shall use any city facility, including access points to Seneca Lake in City shorelines, to launch a hunting or trapping party aimed at killing, trapping or injuring the Seneca Lake*

Monster or any of its descendants. Possession of the carcass of said creatures, or any live creature meeting this description will be considered presumptive evidence of a violation of this section." The penalty for violating the law is up to $250, 15 days in jail or both.

Further to west is the much smaller and shallower Silver Lake, outside the town of Perry in Wyoming County. When Native American villages dotted the shore and countryside, they would not fish in the waters of the lake. It was believed that a mysterious and dangerous monster "as big as a flour barrel" lived below the surface.

The first reported sighting of the Silver Lake Serpent by a settler was on July 13, 1855. Four fishermen were ready to call it a day after spending hours out on the water. They watched what they thought was a log float by until it suddenly started to move in unlog-like ways, undulating from side to side like a snake. The creature then leapt from the water, plunged back in and disappeared. Some of the fishermen claimed that the serpent was sixty-feet long and had red glowing red eyes, like the monster later reported to inhabit Loch Ness in Scotland.

The Silver Lake Sea Serpent as it appeared on a antique postcard.

Between July 13th and the end of the summer season that year, over one hundred people also reported to have seen the creature. The chance to catch a glimpse of the Silver Lake Serpent drew people to the lakeshore from hundreds of miles away. Newspapers around the country fed their readers' curiosity by carrying stories about the sightings. With the coming of each summer season came renewed interest in the serpent. An influx of curious tourists meant more money for the local businesses, especially the Walker Hotel owned by Artemus B. Walker, who had a vested interest in the Silver Lake Sea Serpent. Just how much would soon come to light.

The Walker Hotel was the victim of fire on December 19, 1857. After the fire was extinguished the firemen walked through the building to assess the damage, and it was then that the identity of the serpent was discovered. In the attic of the hotel was the "carcass" of the beast. It consisted of a large pile of canvas and a wire frame shaped like the serpent. Walker confessed that he had come up with scheme to create the sea serpent to bring more people to the lake and drum up business for his hotel and the local merchants. It was an idea that came to him after hearing the old Native American legend. Artemus Walker left town in shame and moved to Canada for a few years after the town found out that he was behind the hoax. When enough time passed and the people seemed to forget about it, Walker moved back to Silver Lake and rebuilt his hotel.

A flashback article in the June 16, 1976 issue of the Latrobe Bulletin from Latrobe, Pennsylvania said Truman Gillett and AB Walker *"constructed the serpent from waterproof canvas, paint and wire. Forced air through a hose connected to the monster caused it to surface and ropes were used to tow it to various corners of the lake's shoreline."*

Some papers around the time of the first sighting, and after it was discovered to be a hoax, made light of the sea serpent even though many believed it to be real. The Buffalo Daily Republic ran the following story on June 15, 1858. *"We have just received the startling intelligence, says the Toledo Blade, via tow-line telegraph from Ogdensburg that the veritable Sea Serpent last seen in Silver Lake has again appeared! He has just been seen by two sailors through a glass, among the thousand islands of the St. Lawrence. The glass was in the form of a bottle and held about a quart."*

Hoax or not, the Silver Lake Sea Serpent drew hundreds, if not thousands of people to the lakeshore, boosting the economy. Beginning in 1952, the Jaycees of Perry recreated the serpent for the annual Silver Lake Sea Serpent Festival. Their serpent was ironically destroyed by fire, as were the two others that have been built since.

Silver Lake Sea Serpent #3 in 1962. Like all the serpents before, and the one after, it was destroyed by a fire while in storage.

Lily Dale

Western New York was referred to as a burned-over district as part of the Second Great Awakening because a "spiritual fervor seemed to set the area on fire." Religions and social movements began here, spanning across the state from the Finger Lakes all the way to the shores of Lake Erie. Mormonism was founded by Joseph Smith in an orchard in Palmyra, while Spiritualism first came about in the rural home of the Fox Sisters near Newark. The Women's Rights Movement began in Seneca Falls in 1848. Perhaps the most unique places to come from the burned-over district were the intellectual/spiritual summer communities such as the Methodist camps of Chautauqua Lake and Silver Lake Institutes, as well as the Spiritualist community at Lily Dale near Jamestown.

Lily Dale was not the first Spiritualist community, but it is one of the few which have survived the last century and a half. Although it is agreed that the Spiritualist Movement started with the Hydesville manifestations on the Fox farm in 1848, the seeds were planted a few years earlier. A mesmerist by the name of Dr. Moran spoke to a group of people in Laona, New York near present day Lily Dale. During the lecture, they received messages from "the Spirit," including how to lay hands on the faithful in order to heal them. The spark created in Laona was fanned into a flame with the events at Hydesville and the group began calling themselves Spiritualists. Mediums and other faithful members of the church descended on Laona and in 1850, the Laona Free Association was formed, five years later it became the First Spiritualist Society of Laona.

Jeremiah Carter attended Dr. Moran's lecture in 1844, in fact his physical ailments were cured when hands were laid on him.

Ever since, he was convinced that he was receiving messages from the Spirit. One such message instructed Carter to build a camp meeting ground on the farmland owned by William Alden. In 1879 the Alden land was purchased to create what would become the Lily Dale Assembly (*ronngy.net: History of Lily Dale*). When it was first opened, it was known as the Cassadaga Free Thinkers, whose main purpose was to promote the connection between science, philosophy and Spiritualism. In 1906, after a few name changed, the community finally became the Lily Dale Assembly. The first religious service at Lily Dale was held in the Bough House, which was a canopy of branches entwined with flowers that stood in a clearing in the Leolyn Woods surrounded by log benches.

Vintage post card of the grounds at the Lily Dale Assembly. (source: author's private collection)

Over the years the community of Lily Dale has grown, today having around 1,600 cottages, two hotels, bookstores, restaurants, a library and museum. One hotel is of interest, both architecturally and spiritually (as you will later learn). The structure which would later become the Maplewood Hotel was built in 1880. I call it a structure because it was first used as a barn and stable for horses on the Alden farm. The construction is "hung suspension," which means that when an expansion is needed, specifically an additional floor, the entire building is raised up and the new floor is built underneath. Even though the magnificent building came from humble beginnings, it continues to offer guests a taste of Victorian elegance that was offered at the turn of the 20th century. One of its most striking features is a beautiful oversized porch that has a breathtaking view of Cassadaga Lake. Although Lily Dale is filled with mediums and the Spirit, the Maplewood Hotel is a sanctuary for meditation and peace, so much so that in the lobby of the hotel hangs a sign which reads "No Seances, Readings or Healings Allowed."

The Fox Sisters' home as it sat on the Lily Dale Assembly property. Pilgrims from around the world visited it to pay homage to the birthplace of Spiritualism. (source: author's private collection)

The connection between Lily Dale and the Fox Sisters remained strong even after the deaths of Margaret and Kate. The original Fox home, and the site of the famous manifestations, in Hydesville was donated to Lily Dale and moved there in 1915 as an important monument. Spiritualists flocked to Lily Dale to pay homage to the sacred place where their religion began. A mysterious fire destroyed the house on September 21, 1955. Only two objects survived the flames; the Fox family Bible and an old trunk. It is believed that the trunk was once owned by Charles Rosna, the peddler murdered in the house in 1843 and buried in the basement wall. The spirit of the peddler was on of the first to communicate with Margaret and Kate Fox in the spring of 1848.

"Lily Dale had comforted the bereaved, demonstrated the truth of immortality, and shown others a way of life known as the religion of Spiritualism." The community has always pushed three main character points; sobriety, humility and no showmanship, while trying to emphasize to those visit the mediums that everyone has free will, our futures are not set in stone. *"More than a folk belief in ghosts, Spiritualism was and is a structured belief that humans consist of a body, a soul and a spirit. When someone dies, the soul and the spirit live on in a spirit realm. (Journal of Religion 1930)."* *"The chief duty of those spirits is to look after the welfare and progress of those on Earth* (Lily Dale Where Living and Dead Reconnect)." Greg Newkirk in 2015 better explains the premise of Spiritualism with this quote – *"The basic premise behind Spiritualism is simple; no one really leaves when they die, and death is simply a change of state. If the living are melting ice cubes, the dead are just the water. As such, the deceased can be 'refrozen' for a time to interact with the living, whether it be for a comforting chat, a bit of advice, or even just as a fun trick at parties."*

As stated before, Lily Dale is filled to the brim with spirits. Not all the spirits are ghosts, though there are a few roaming around. Going back to its roots, the ghosts of two horses can be heard running on the third (formerly main) floor of the Maplewood Hotel (Galloping Ghosts of Lily Dale 8/1/2015). A Victorian-era bearded gentleman wearing wire rim glasses appears in the assembly hall. And at night, particularly near Inspiration Stump, Leolyn Woods become overrun with elementals and spirits. Hazy figures are often seen in the moonlight as well as mysterious lights.

Newark State School

When the Newark State School first opened in 1878, it was called a satellite location for the Syracuse State School, called the Newark Custodial Institution for Developmentally Disabled, Childbearing Women. Wow! That's a mouthful! The main objective of the institution was to have a place for girls too old to accommodate at the Syracuse State Institution for Feeble-Minded Children, but not mentally stable enough to be sent out into the world on their own. After women reached menopause, they were sent back to their home county for treatment. An interesting fact; the definition of "feeble-minded" during the Victorian period was not very specific and meant someone that had a high-functioning level of developmental disability or mental deficiency, but it could also include women with loose moral values. As with most mental institutions of the time, there was a very broad spectrum of reasons for a woman to be committed; for asthma to superstition to novel reading and laziness.

The institution went through several name changes throughout the years that it was in operation. As often as the name changed, its main objective evolved over time as well. In 1885 it became the State Custodial Asylum for Feeble-Minded women and was no longer linked to the Syracuse State School. At the time it was large enough to accommodate 600 girls. By February 1913, the school was beyond capacity with 795 women residing there and another 235 on the waiting list. The name changed again to the Newark State School for Mental Directives in 1919. A few years later, girls as young as five could be admitted. 1927 brought the final name change, becoming the Newark State School. Up until the end of 1931, only females were admitted to the institution. On February 17, 1932 boys could attend for the first time.

Many of the buildings on the Newark State School campus have sat empty for decades. The Hillcrest Residence is just one of them.

As with most institutions of the time, the patients or inmates (as they were referred to because they usually were not there of their own free will) were not humanly treated. Many were treated like animals, some chained to the wall or kept in cages. The living conditions were less than ideal, often not meeting the most basic of human needs. It is safe to say that they had a miserable existence once they were committed. Very few cases of abuse were brought to light, and those that were reported were generally swept under the rug. Rarely was a doctor or staff member charged with a crime. This little gem was gleaned from the January 3, 1900 issue of the Rochester Democrat and Chronicle. The resignation of the resident doctor at the State Custodial School for Feeble-Minded Women, Dr. Alice Brownell was asked for after an investigation into the treatment of the women cared for at the institution. Brownell was charged with cruelty and the harsh treatment of women, which at times was so brutal that marks were left on their bodies.

The case of Mary Lake shows the lengths gone to in order to cover up the mistreatment of the girls at the school. Lake, along with other inmates who had no determinable mental issues, were adamant on leaving the institution to testify to authorities about what really went on behind closed doors. The plan was discovered by an administrator at the State School and a letter was sent to the Commissioner of Charities that was meant to discredit any testimony that Mary Lake and the others would give. The letter read – *Mary Lake has had a number of attacks of excitement, but none so severe as the present attacks, nor did they last as long. She has been very much worse the last two weeks. I have no doubt of her insanity.*

There were other women so determined to leave the Newark State School and escape what they surely felt as their personal hell that they would go to any lengths to het out. Not many were successful in their bid for freedom. One story about an escape attempt was reported in the Springville Journal on April 27, 1893. *"Julia Littman...daughter of a perfumer...punished for some offense by the matron standing upon her prostrate body, with one foot upon her throat and the other upon her stomach...unable to stand the treatment longer, she jumped from the second story window, falling upon the pavement, receiving severe bruising and disfiguring her face."*

From 1878 until the State School closed in 1991, over 110 years, hundreds of people died within those brick walls, mainly of illness and disease, but also from unnatural causes as well. The institution used two cemeteries, at least to this author's knowledge, to hold the earthly remains of those who died there and were unclaimed after death, a cemetery right on the property of the State School's farm as well as a portion of the East Newark Cemetery that was designated for inmate burials.

The campus of the institution followed the cottage plan with multiple buildings. When the Newark State School closed, come of the buildings were repurposed while others have been closed for nearly thirty years. The appearance of those buildings portrays a picture of what classic horror movies are based on. The walls have peeling paint, while antiquated medical equipment is strewn about. People who have found themselves in the buildings alone claim to have experienced things that they cannot explain. They caught glimpses of figures sitting in rooms that have been unoccupied for decades. Echoes of sobbing and unintelligible rants are heard throughout the halls. Wheelchairs are even known to roll around on their own.

Rathbone's Ghost

William Harrington, William Allen and Floyd Myers had spent much of December 24, 1896 drinking. While in a drunken state, Harrington and Allen accused Myers of stealing a buffalo robe. Angered by the accusation, Myers pulled out a gun and shot them both. Harrington died within minutes and Allen breathed his last the following day. Floyd fled the scene of the brutal murders, evading arrest for almost 48 hours. The blood-soaked cabin along the Erie Railroad tracks offered a perfect setting for the story of a vengeful spirit.

The Steuben County town of Rathbone once had a "ghost" which terrified men until a group of women set things straight. Sometimes a ghost is the spirit of the dead and sometimes what e think of as a ghost is much more than it appears. The Star Gazette from Elmira published an account of the entire events on November 4, 1897.

Rathbone's Ghost

Appeared at Night Before Murderer Myers Shanty Frightened the Sports

Numerous Blood Curdling Stories Which Have Been Afloat Regarding It – a Party of Rathbone's Fair Daughters Routed His Ghostship

Rathbone has a ghost, or rather it had one. The house was known as the Donivan Shanty, formerly occupied by Murderer Myers, which was the scene of the awful tragedy, last Christmas Eve, has since been occupied, except by a number of the sporting element of the quiet town of Rathbone, who have been in the habit gathering there Sundays and playing cards and sometimes the game extended far into the night, but of late a ghost has appeared upon the scene, and has scared off the would-be card sharps.

A peddler struck the town one night recently, and he expressed a desire to mix-up a game of draw. He was told of the spook haunted shanty which was the only place where the game could be conducted, but as he was not afraid of any old ghost, the sports went to the shanty. The game started and had just begun to wax hot when the white-robed figure was slowly patrolling up and down in front of the shanty and groaning in a dismal manner, and the sports all took to their heels except the poor peddler, who was too scared to run, he succeeded however, in grabbing hold of the coat tails of one of the players, and he having an important engagement elsewhere at the moment, had no time to tarry, therefore he left the coat tails in the peddler's hand. Since then no one dared to go near the shanty after nightfall, and stories concerning the ghost grew numerous, bone-shaking and blood-freezing. Things went on in this way for some time, until finally, according to the Addison Advertiser, a party composed of a number of Rathbone's fair damsels who had become disgusted with the stories of the ghost, conceived the idea of visiting the shanty at night and routing his ghostship. Armed with sticks, stones, etc., they went to the shanty and awaited the appearance of the ghost, and their vigil was soon rewarded, the ghost appearing in front of the house, they rushed upon him, pelting him with stones and beating him with clubs. He (the ghost) considered discretion the better part of valor, so discarding the sheet, he ran away, but not without receiving many bruises, caused by the blows administered by the girls. It is necessary to say that there is a lot of young men and some old ones, too, ho feel very cheap, as well as they might, over the routing of the ghost. The poker game still flourishes.

Rochester Fata Morgana

One of the most famous mirages in history is the sightings of the Flying Dutchman, a ghost ship which was a harbinger of death that had been witnessed by sailors around the world for centuries. A fata morgana is a mirage, an atmospheric phenomena, in a complex form which is usually seen on or just above the horizon. The shores of Lake Ontario have been the setting for fantastic fata morganas, including the Rochester Mirage in 1871 and the 1894 Buffalo Mirage.

At the highest point in Mt. Hope Cemetery there was a wooden observation town called the Fandango, which unfortunately is no longer standing. It was a popular destination for visitors at the cemetery. Remember that Mt. Hope Cemetery was a park as much as a burial ground. People took picnic lunches on the graves as well as strolled along the paths that winded through the rolling hills that made up the grounds. The tower drew plenty of visitors each day, but being a Sunday with a bright clear sky, there were many more people at the Fandango than usual for a spring day. People climbed the tower to get a breathtaking view of downtown Rochester and Lake Ontario. However, on April 16, 1871 they witnessed a once in a lifetime event.

Instead of catching a glimpse of the Rochester skyline, Canadian landmarks and her beautiful countryside were laid out before them as clear as day even though there were more than 50 miles between them. Word about the strange vision traveled fast and by the afternoon a crowd of more than a thousand spectators gathered to witness the Rochester mirage.

The following excerpt is from a published witness account of the mirage.

As if suddenly by a great tidal wave, old Lake Ontario had burst her confines and buried the entire north part of the city; and where generally thousands of buildings and churches are visible, nothing but the blue waves of the lake could be seen...Away to the right and left, as far as the eye could see, was the Canada coast (where) could be seen her shores, studded with mountains, hills, valleys, inland bays and lakes, rivers and forests; and so perfect at times that the sun's rays, shining on the barren sand cliffs, would illuminate their sides like dazzling mountains of glass.

The event was talked about around the country, in fact the Rochester Mirage story was featured in the May 13, 1871 issue of Frank Leslie's Illustrated.

A few days later, the event made national headlines in the Richmond Dispatch on April 21, 1871.

The reader can form some idea of its grandeur by knowing that a country separated from Rochester by a lake seventy to one hundred miles in width was, as if suddenly, by the great hand of its creator, painted upon the heavens so plain to be seen from a standing point one hundred miles distant. Gentlemen present who were familiar with the Canada shore could readily distinguish Rice Lake, Belvedere, and other prominent points in Canada. The lake looked as though it had by a great tidal wave rolled upon Rochester, had covered one entire half of the city, as no building could be seen north of Main Street, or any land between the city and the lake.

On the morning of August 16, 1894, the residents of Buffalo woke up to a similar and extraordinary mirage. The city of Toronto, which was 56 miles away, appeared to be right next door. The harbor, downtown church steeples and even a side-wheel paddle steamer from Rochester could be seen on the horizon. Unlike the 1871 mirage in Rochester, this one only lasted about an hour. However, the country-wide coverage was greater.

The following quote about the Buffalo Mirage appeared in the August 18, 1894 edition of the Morning News from Wilmington, Delaware.

"...those who first witnessed the phenomenon were able to count the church spires in the Canadian city. The phenomenon is classed by natural scientists as a mirage of the third order...showed the entire breadth of Lake Ontario, a projection east of the mirrored Toronto being easily recognized as Charlotte, a suburb of Rochester. In a direct line between this point and Toronto Bay a large side-wheel steamer could be seen making her way. The vessel was the Norseman...A sailboat, apparently a yacht, was the most distinct of all objects. Her mainsail was set, and she was lying close to the wind. She was seen to turn and careen with the west wind, and then suddenly disappear, as though nature had removed a slide from her magic lantern.

In the same way the whole great scene began slowly to dissolve, a bank of black clouds sweeping along and obliterating the picture to the disappointment of thousands who had swarmed to the tops of the highest buildings...they were able to discover the outlines of all the streets of Toronto, and declared that a better view of the city could not be had without approaching within ten miles of it.

Tavern on the Hill

The Tavern on the Hill was a public house on Swamp Road in the town of Sweden at the western end of Monroe County. The tavern, even though on a road that was somewhat isolated, at one time drew a hefty business from stagecoaches that traveled along present-day Lake Road which connected the Ridge to the Buffalo roads.

The tavern itself was two stories tall, with the ballroom on the second floor and the bar in the basement. There were also rooms that were rented to weary travelers. Guests would come together in the bar after their evening meal to drink and share stories, even tell a few tall tales. Occasionally things would get out of hand, one thing would lead to another and a fight would break out. One fight ended in the murder of a peddler. It was the ghost of the peddler that is said to have been the cause of the Tavern of the Hill's demise.

Travelers were convinced that the peddler's spirit returned to the tavern every night, a few even had encounters with the ghost. One man claimed that the peddler's ghost woke him up around midnight to open the door so he could get out. The next morning there was a knock on the window – the ghost wanted to get back in. Another guest told about how the spirit of the peddler left the Tavern on the Hill at midnight to make his sales calls, always returning with an empty sample case when day broke.

Tales of the peddler haunting the tavern quickly spread and travelers looked for lodging someplace else. No one wanted to risk running in to a ghost. Eventually there would be no guests staying the night, and even the barroom grew quiet. The peddler's ghost had scared all the business away. The property sold at auction and remained closed for several years before a man from Europe reopened it. No matter what the man did, the peddler's ghost showed him time and time again who was truly in charge and it finally closed for good.

    Empty and abandoned, a local farmer used the old tavern to store his crop. Due to the unconventional use of the tavern and the harsh winters that Western New York tends to endure, the tavern slowly began to deteriorate. Stones were taken from the building to repair the foundations of surrounding homes. All that remains today of the Tavern on the Hill are a few pieces of its stone wall hidden in the overgrowth.

The Cobblestone Inn

On Route 104 between Rochester and Niagara Fall in Oak Orchard-on-the-Ridge (part of the town of Ridgeway) is the historic Cobblestone Inn. During the 1800s, the Ridge was a major stagecoach route connecting flourishing towns with the, at the time, wilds of the west. The large stone inn provided food and accommodations for wary travelers as well as water for the horses.

Zaccariah Spencer built the 6,200 square foot building in 1837. When it was finished, the inn was the largest cobblestone building in North America and was known as the Spencer House. He passed the building and the business down to his son Henry in 1843. Henry Spencer was a loner, who never married or had children, which was rare at the time. But he was a very successful businessman. Two years later he committed suicide inside the inn. There was no obituary or record of Henry's burial, except for a document deeding the property back to Zaccariah. The deed simply stated that Henry Spencer's death was by his own device.

The death of Henry wasn't the end of the story of the Spencer family and the inn. Zaccariah once again passed the property down, this time to his two sons Burrll and Samuel. This decision was no better than the previous. Samuel and Burrll were not businessmen by any means and they quickly ran the Cobblestone Inn into bankruptcy. Additionally, Burrll was accused and convicted of forging checks in the sum of $6,000,000 in today's money. Spencer's sons lost inn and their story ends here.

There are claims that a now collapsed tunnel ran from the basement of the Cobblestone Inn east to the bank of Oak

Orchard Creek. Through the tunnel, it is said that runaway slaves and sugar were smuggled into the inn.

At 6,200 square feet, the Cobblestone Inn built in 1837 is the largest cobblestone structure in North America.

Violent and tragic death would call again not far the Cobblestone Inn's doorstep, this time a much more violent death than that of Henry. A neighboring farm was owned by the Grimes family who were very prosperous, being able to employ several farm hands. The patriarch of the family had hired a hand by the name of Eugene Emory. Emory had fallen in love with the farmer's fourteen-year old daughter Cora and a close friendship developed. It was clear that she did not have the same feelings for the man that was more than twenty years her senior. When Cora told Eugene that the relationship would go no further, he became enraged. Eugene followed Cora into the house and picked up a piece of firewood. On June 24, 1889, he hit Cora in the head several times with the log while she screamed for help, ultimately bashing in her skull. Her little brother tried but couldn't get into the house to save her and soon the screams stopped. Cora was dead and her murderer escaped. A posse was formed to hunt Eugene Emory down. Knowing that if the posse caught him, he would probably be lynched, Eugene tuned himself in. Eugene Emory was quotes as saying "She was the dearest, sweetest girl" and that he loved her, but killed her because "she was ugly to me." Emory's attorney pled insanity at his trial, but that defense did not work. He was convicted of second-degree murder on February 13, 1890 and sentenced to life in prison. It turned out to be a death sentenced because about a decade after his imprisonment, he died in his cell.

Those at the Cobblestone Inn, which has been converted into a duplex, have seen shadow figures and apparitions. It continues to be an inn for spirits traveling along the haunted highway. There have also been paranormal experiences that could be attributed to Cora and her attacker. More than one person has reported that they heard a loud panicked and painful scream of a woman and doors slamming shut.

The Ghost of Glenwood Cemetery

A short piece appeared in the Buffalo Review published on November 19. 1900.

The laborers who were working on the Buffalo and Lockport electric railroad's new freight line, in the rear of Glenwood Cemetery, declare that Saturday night, when working about their big fire they saw the glare reflected upon a mysterious figure, which glided about among the graves, and seemed to gain an entrance to the famous Castlemaine vault. It did not reappear.

The granite mausoleum was originally built for Frederick Castlemaine who married Isabella Sutherland, one of the famous Seven Sutherland Sisters and fifteen years his senior. The sisters were the daughters of Fletcher and Mary Sutherland. They appeared with the Barnum and Bailey Circus as a side show in the late 1800s. Their claim to fame – 37' of hair between all of the girls. When Frederick died, he was very young, just around 29 years old.

In March 1898, the mausoleum was broken into, the trespassers came with one of two intentions; to either steal the body and hold it for ransom (why not? He had a famous wife) or to rob the corpse of any valuables that Frederick may have been buried with. They first tried to come through the inside door using powder and dynamite, but to no avail. It didn't deter them though; the men were able to gain access through the back window. According to an article in the Lockport Journal with the GRAVE ROBBERS MOLEST THE DEAD, "the robbers opened the outer box in which incased the coffin containing the remains of the later Frederick H. Castlemaine and pried open the top of the casket. They searched carefully for valuables which they evidently expected to find in the coffin but there were none." After searching every nook and cranny in the vault, they came up empty handed. But the robbers were determined to walk away with something for their trouble, so they made off with the heavy bronze front door. No one was ever arrested in connection to the attempted grave robbery and theft.

Perhaps the specter seen by fire light by the railroad men was the ghost of Frederick H. Castlemaine, wandering about the cemetery after his eternal slumber was disturbed by the molestation of the grave robbers.

The Ghost of Horseshoe Lake

Let me set the scene. The lake is so calm that the surface is a smooth as glass. A boy and a girl sit next to each other in a rowboat under a brilliant canopy of stars. The music that was wafting over the water from the dance hall on shore has gone silent and they are now serenaded by the crickets and cicadas. It is a perfect night for a little midnight necking. Then a mist forms above the water slowly taking a human shape. According to the July 10, 1923 edition of the Buffalo Enquirer, this exact scenario happened at Horseshoe Lake in Batavia.

The two parties had just pulled up into the little cove east of the bathing beach and were pondering on the mysteries of the heavens, the stillness of the night, the music at the dance hall across the way having ceased and partaking of the atmosphere which suggested mystery, and weirdly things, when suddenly a light appeared and floated about a dozen feet above the water of the lake. Wifts of clouds veiled the scattered stars and a moist, clammy wind was moving over the black surface of the lake...

Needless to say the mood was ruined They quickly took their boats ashore and told the workers at the resort of their harrowing experience. A similar encounter had been reported by two boys fishing off Long Pine Point along the western shore of Horseshoe Lake some time earlier.

Over the years several other eyewitness accounts had been recorded with similar details regarding the human-shaped white mist that hovers above the surface of the lake. People who have seen the ghost at Horseshoe Lake, and even those who have just heard the stories, believe that it is the spirit of one of the people who had died in the water. Throughout the years at least three, maybe more, have died there.

First there was John Gould, a twenty-year-old young man who had drowned on July 7, 1912. Gould, an expert swimmer, spent many summers swimming in Horseshoe Lake. On the day of his death he was attempting to swim across the lake and back, which he had done many times. When Gould was in the middle of the lake on his return lap something went horribly wrong. He was struck by a swimmer's cramp or a sudden illness came over him that caused him to quickly sink below the surface. Two bystanders tried to save the young man, but he expired before they could get him to shore.

July 24, 1920, eight years later, fourteen-year-old Max Gressinger died in the lake. The boy was disabled by a crippling leg deformity. This ailment was most likely responsible for his death. Max had been camping by Horseshoe Lake and went swimming with the other children at the campground when tragedy struck. He was in water too deep for him to handle and he discovered he was in trouble and began struggling to keep his head above water, but eventually sank out of sight. The groundskeeper tried to rescue the boy and pulled him to shore. For two hours police worked to revive Max, but it was without success.

The third death was perhaps the most heartbreaking. Norma Teffner, a twenty-one-year-old Sunday school teacher, laid her clothes out on the beach, walked into the water and drowned herself in Horseshoe Lake on September 8, 1922. A suicide note was found tucked into her clothes after her body was recovered. It read as follows.

You boys listen to Pa and you will come out all right. Have your eyes and nose taken care of with my money in the bank. Be sure to mind Pa. Since my hair is gone my looks are gone too and it makes me so nervous.

Norma had recently had her hair cut into a fashionable bob. However, the new hairstyle required her beautiful curls to be cut off, which was a decision that she soon regretted, and it drove her into a deep depression. She felt that the only way she could relieve herself of it was to end her life.

With so many lives of young people tragically taken in Horseshoe Lake, it is no surprise that a spirit or two remains. But which one's spirit makes the midnight appearance will never be known.

Vintage image of the eastern shore of Horseshoe Lake in Batavia, Genesee County.

The Jockey's Ghost

Jockey Danny Macklin of Detroit, Michigan was riding his horse around the local track when it was overcome with a violent fit. The horse took off like a shit and threw Macklin to the ground. He struck his head on a rock which left a hole in his temple and a trail of blood trickling down his cheek, killing him instantly. The ghost of Danny Macklin had reportedly appeared at racetracks across the country looking for the horse that killed him.

Rochester Driving Park and the park's entrance from Dewey Avenue.

Macklin's spirit manifested at the Driving Park, which at the time was a horse track. The incident was relayed in a detailed article in the Democrat and Chronicle on August 19, 1890. The following is the actual article in its entirety.

A Terrifying Specter That Was Seen as the Driving Park

The mystic hour when church yards are popularly supposed to yawn like a reporter on 'long watch' has no terror or the average Rochestarian, who feels as easy and safe at midnight as at mid-day. But rarely is a real ghost heard of here, there are people even in this city so constituted that they can recount tales of personal encounters with uncanny specters that are calculated to make a timid man's hair stand on end.

It has recently been reported about in the Third Ward, that the little cottage, just off Plymouth Avenue, that was once the home of the Stoddards, is now inhabited by a ghost that walked nightly and there are imaginative people who actually think that they have seen a ghost.

But another part of the city boasts of a ghost that within a week has scared a dozen people. The people in question were grooms and jockeys who have had charge of the horses at the Driving Park during the past week, and the story told is quite interesting. The grooms who had charge of the flyers slept at night in the temporary bunks erected in the stables, in order to watch and care for the horses. The grooms divided the night into watches.

Last Thursday night the men who took the midnight watch had just relieved their companions and were quietly chatting in front of the stable, when one espied a curious white object near a clump of trees. At first, he thought it was a trick of the moon and paid no attention to it. As it shifted about, he thought perhaps – well, he didn't know what to think, so he just sat still and watched. The white object moved out of the clump of trees and went to the stable. At that instant the other watchman saw the object. The apparition was then at once recognized as a ghost. Its clothes were white but not whiter than its blanched face. Down one cheek ran a blood red line. Both watchmen were paralyzed with fright and could neither move nor speak. Their limbs refused to act, and their senses were benumbed.

Straight into the stables walked the ghost. One door was open, but the specter preferred to pass through another that was closed. As it disappeared into the stable and they plucked up a little courage and keeping close together stole inside after it. The ghost was slowly pacing up and down in front of the stalls. Apparently, it was examining the horses. It suddenly occurred to the men that perhaps they were being tricked, that the ghost might be a man who meant to harm the horses. They gave the alarm and the sleeping jockeys jumped up to their feet half awake, and they too saw the apparition. The ghost paid no attention to the noise and bustle but kept examining the horses, which themselves became alarmed at the noise and began neighing and stamping.

The men became more and more terrified, until one who had more courage than the rest started for the specter with a pitchfork. Then the specter judiciously vanished. They saw nothing more that night nor after it. The jockeys say that the ghost was a genuine one, and that they recognized the features as those of a jockey who was killed in Detroit some years ago and who, as legend goes, haunted the racing stables looking for the horse that killed him. What particular indigestibility the men had for supper on the night in question had not yet been learned.

The Peddler

In late March 1848, not long after the Fox family moved into their home in Hydesville, "it" began. An occasional knock here and there that quickly intensified into a fury of knocks and mysterious noises that kept the family awake at night. The activity usually centered around the bedroom of the two teenage sisters, Margaret and Kate. In order to communicate with the spirit (or spirits), the curious sisters came up with a system of raps to get answers to questions they would ask. They identified two spirits in the house who they referred to as Mr. Splitfoot, another name for the Devil, and a murdered peddler. The life experiences, as well as the rise and fall of the Fox Sisters are well documented in books and newspaper articles, but little is known about the peddler's life and death other than what is said about the original rapping events in 1848. In my research, I have found articles from 1848 and 1904 that relate directly to the peddler; his life, death and ghost.

It is said that no little excitement prevails at Arcadia, Wayne County, NY, in regards to an underground arrangement, in which it is supposed some discontented inhabitant of the otherworld had a hand. The story goes, according to the 'City Items' of the Geneva Gazette, that a servant girl having some errand in the cellar of the house, on crossing the ground floor perceived a portion to give way beneath her feet, and at the same time heard a loud rap. The man of the house was called, and on proceeding to the spot the same supernatural rap was heard, and the 'hole in ground' perfectly visible. On putting the inquiry, 'Is there anyone buried down here?' it was answered by the same unearthly rap. 'Was he murdered?' received the same reply. 'How long have you been here?' was answered with five raps, supposed to indicate five years. Other questions were asked, and answers given in the same mysterious way. Picks, bars and spades were procured, and at it they went, to relieve the murdered man from confinement.

At the depth of about four feet gushed a stream of water, filling the hole almost to the top. On attempting to bail it, they were unable to tower it more than a foot. On thrusting a bar down two feet below the bottom of the hole, it struck against a board; but no further discoveries have been made. Hundreds are flocking to the spot, and stories are already afloat of a peddler having been missing from the region some years since, and the suspicion rests upon a man in that vicinity as a murderer! This is a great world, and the present month peculiarly prolific in wonderful discoveries (Jeffersonian Republican, April 27, 1848).

The Fox family home in Hydesville, NY. (source: author's private collection)

Several families lived in the home at 1510 Hydesville Road before the Fox family moved in, including the Bells, who rented the house from 1842 to 1843. Coincidently, a peddler by the name of Charles B. Rosna disappeared during the Bells' residency. Rosna's last stop as a door-to-door salesman and his life was the Bell household. Through the process of interviews with neighbors and the servant girl who worked for the Bell family, Mrs. Bell was the last person to see Rosna alive and had come into possession of several new and expensive items. Though she denied having any knowledge of his disappearance or demise. Shortly after the peddler's visit to the house, terrifying knocks and sounds that seemed to be coming from the floorboards were heard by the Bell's servant. Mrs. Bell, in order to stop further investigation quickly dismissed them as being the sounds of rats and even went as far as buying rat poison to corroborate the story. The noises continued, becoming unbearable to tolerate and the Bell family was forced to move out.

The excitement in reference to the mysterious knocking in a house at Hydesville, Wayne County, still continues, and the revelations which it makes daily, are astonishing the multitude. A pamphlet had been published, containing a great number of certificates from individuals residing in the neighborhood, who have heard the mysterious knocking, and have propounded to his ghostship a variety of questions, all of which have been answered by raps.

The occupant of the house is named John D. Fox, who formerly resided in Rochester, and himself and he wife both make a certificate in regard to the mysterious thumping.

They state that they first heard the noise about the 30th of March, in the evening, just after the family had retired to rest, and this is continued from that time to the present. The ghost not only answered all the questions put to it, but readily gives the age of each child in the family, and of others in the neighborhood but the 'spirits' history of its own affairs is altogether marvelous. The 'story of its wrongs' runs somewhat like thus:

It states the body it once inhabited was that of a peddler, that *it was 31 years of age, and was murdered about four years since by the then occupant of the house by having its throat cut with a butcher knife; this is left a family of five children, two sons and three daughters, who are now living in Orleans County; that its wife died about two years since; that the amount of money taken was $500, besides a trunk and pack of goods; that the wife of the man who committed the murder had gone away that night, as well as a girl who worked there, named Lucretia Pulver; that it was murdered on a Tuesday night at 12 o'clock; that the first letter of its given name was C, and that of its surname was B, but it refused to give the entire name, (a considerate ghost)!*

...In the course of their questions, it was asked who committed the murder, and each individual was named who had occupied the house from its erection – No knocking was heard until the name of a very respectable man now resides at Lyons, Wayne County, was called, when it made three knocks louder than common, and the bedstead jarred more than it had done before! It states that the murderer cannot be punished because there are no witnesses of his crime, and yet so many are the absurd stories about the matter, that the individual had felt constrained to procure a certificate of good character and respectability, signed by some forty or fifty of his former neighbors.

Thus the matter stands, and what render it still more remarkable is the fact that individuals who have resided there previous to the present occupant taking the premises, now come forward, and over their own signatures certify that they too heard the same mysterious noises when they occupied the premises! According to the unquiet spirit's story it was buried ten feet underground, in a particular part of the cellar designated, and that since, on account of the body affecting the water in a neighboring well, it was removed from its first resting place, and buried on the bank of 'Mud Creek,' more recently known as the 'Ganargwa,' It says that it shall keep up the rapping until remains, a portion of which are still underneath the building, are discovered, and the residents round about have made a vow this his ghostship shall be attended to just as soon as the water in the cellar will permit. – We wait further revelations with a good deal of interest. In the meantime, we trust that the neighborhood will keep 'cool.' And that the ghost of the murdered peddler may continue to make all needful and proper suggestions in reference to the matter (Springville Express May 6, 1848).

William H. Hyde, owner of what was known as the 'Old Spook House,' has discovered human bones under the cellar wall, which had been fallen in as a result of being undermined by running water.

It was in the 'Old Spook House' at Hydesville, Wayne County, NY, that the Fox sisters, daughters of Mr. and Mrs. John D. Fox, started the movement which has resulted in modern Spiritualism.

The Fox family occupied the house in the late forties. In 1848 the family were much disturbed by certain mysterious 'knocks' and 'raps.' It is alleged that at length Kate Fox, one of the two daughters, discovered that the cause of the sounds was intelligent, and that questions asked would be answered by the number of raps, one for 'no' and three for 'yes.'

There is absolutely no doubt that the Fox girls declared that the rappings proceeded from the spirit of a certain peddler, whose throat had been cut by a pervious tenant of the house, and whose body had been buried in the cellar.

An investigation of the matter seemed to show that none of the Fox family produced the rapping. Efforts were made to find the body of the peddler, but they were unsuccessful, probably because of the quantity of running water that was encountered when digging in the cellar was begun (The Evening World November 22m 1904).

According to the Fox sisters' rapping sessions, Charles Rosna's body was stashed somewhere beneath the house. The last family to live at the house in Hydesville was the Fox family. Word spread throughout the countryside about the haunting, and those who missed the neighborhood gossip most certainly read the many accounts that the newspapers were anxious to report. After what the sisters and the family went through, it was impossible for willing occupants to be found. And the house sat empty for more than half a century.

Children would play near the property but were careful not to get too close, stories of a bona fide haunted house and of a body being buried within kept them at bay. Around 1904, a discovery was made that would finally validate the claims of a body being hidden within the wall and the fate of Charles Rosna. Two boys tested their courage and entered the abandoned house, which had been neglected for some time. In a space, exposed by the elements, between a wall in the basement and the foundation were human bones.

Skeptics believe that there is another reason for the bones to be in the basement of the old Fox home. During the 19th century, if a family member died during the winter months when the ground was frozen, the body was interred in the basement until a proper grave could be dug after the spring thaw. They say that perhaps it is a winter burial that never found spring. For those who believe in the otherworld, the bones only affirm that old Charles Rosna communicated beyond his earthly grave in 1848, wishing for his story to be told and his murderer to finally be brought to justice. The fact that the remains were found within the walls, as if was never supposed to be found, supports their theory.

The Screamer of Glen Haven

Dr. James Caleb Jackson turned the Glen Haven House, a hotel along the southern shore of Skaneateles Lake, into the Glen Haven Sanitarium, a water cure, in 1847. It offered luxurious accommodations with a full range of therapeutic services using water from the springs that flowed from the base of the nearby cliffs. The 400-room resort was a popular travel destination that earned accolades in many different publications, including *Summer Excursion Routes – Pennsylvania Railroad Company (1890)*, which describes the resort as follows. "The place has long held the enviable reputation as a summer resort, not only from the healthful situation, but also for the great store of natural beauty at its door." The Glen Haven Sanitarium prided itself on its reputation of being a five-star resort, but it also attracted many rumors about having a dark side along the shore of Skaneateles Lake.

The Glen Haven Sanitarium, it was torn down in the 1930s.

A popular legend says that the sanitarium supposedly burned down in 1912 with the caretaker inside, his agonizing screams piercing the quiet of the lake. His spirit remains and is called "the screamer." He can be heard wailing at night as he paces along the wooded lakeshore. Fact check! The main building of the Glen Haven Sanitarium did burn down (and later rebuilt), but in 1854 with no reported loss of life. That however doesn't discredit the legend of a "screamer." Death would be no stranger to the new resort. Each of the deaths could be the source of the terrifying spectral screams that break the silence of the night.

Lewis Thomas worked at the resort bath house in 1904. For reason that remain unknown, Lewis decided to end his life but the knife he chose was too dull to finish the act. As a result of the suicide attempt, he was committed to the New York State Asylum for the Insane in Ithaca, where he remained confined until his death.

An earlier suicide attempt fifteen years prior to be more successful. Lilliam Dumont ironically had been born and died at Glen Haven, taking her first and last breaths there. She hung herself from the closet doorway in her room with a corset, leaving no note of explanation or consolation for her grieving family. That same week in August 1889, James Terry checked into the resort. James was very sick and knew that his days in this world were numbered. Wishing to be the captain of his own fate, he borrowed a boat and rowed out onto Skaneateles Lake where he jumped overboard and drowned.

The "Screamer" could be any of them, however my vote is for Darius Green. He didn't die at Glen Haven, but across the lake in July 1889. A local newspaper recorded the circumstances of his tragic death. *He was standing on a plank at the side of a large circular saw, greasing the same while it as running at full speed. The plank tipped up and flung him headlong in front of the saw, which cut the top of his head completely off, spilled the brains on the recovered. floor. His left hand was also severed and fell into the lake and has not been recovered.* If that isn't the making of a screaming apparition, I don't know what is.

Van Horn Mansion

James Van Horn moved from New Jersey to Newfane, Niagara County in 1817 with his wife Abigail and their eight children, including his oldest son James Jr. After they arrived, he ran a successful grist mill as well as holding a powerful political offices. When the town of Newfane was founded, the very first meeting was held at the Van Horn Mansion, which James built in 1923. The mansion remained in the Van Horn family until the last ancestor sold it in 1910. The property is not under the care of the Newfane Historical Society, which was passed from owner to owner six times before they acquired it. Part of the reason it changed hands so frequently was because of the ghostly apparitions that wander the halls of the mansion and its grounds. One of the ghosts is said to be that of Malinda Van Horn, the young bride of James Jr.

When the couple married in 1836, Malinda was only twenty years old. Who knew the one year later she would be buried in the cold ground. There is a great deal of mystery surrounding her death, which has led to many theories. It is greatly speculated that she died in childbirth, however there is no record of the couple having a child. It has also been said that she died from a brief illness or a tree fell on Malinda causing her death. There were more scandalous hypotheses as to her death that had tongues wagging among the neighborhood gossips. They believed that she committed suicide, her husband James pushed her down the stairs, or James and his father worked together to poison Malinda. But perhaps the best theory of them all was that she had been caught in bed with a servant and her husband killed her in a fit of anger. A birth certificate was found in California for a baby that had been born the same date as the supposed Van Horn baby and was also born in Newfane, New York. However, the mother listed on the document was not Malinda Van Horn. Conspiracy theorists looking for a juicy tale to fuel the haunting think that the baby was indeed Malinda's, but not fathered by James Jr. When her husband discovered that the child was the product of an illicit affair, he murdered his wife. He then gave the baby to one of the servants, had a fraudulent birth certificate made and sent the "mother" and child to the new territory of California.

    Whatever the cause of death, the family must have been concerned about the suspicion and controversy it would raise or the shame her death would have brought, because Malinda was quickly and quietly buried in a plot on the mansion grounds.

    In the 1950s, the graves in the family cemetery on the grounds were moved to Glenwood Cemetery. All but Malinda's. After being missing for decades, her headstone was finally found stashed in the shed, but the location of her final resting place remained a mystery until 1992. A cadaver dog was brought in to assist in the search and her remains were recovered. Malinda was reburied in the rose garden and reunited with her headstone, which had been inscribed so long ago with these loving words:

> *Sleep, Malinda, sleep.*
> *Where flowers bloom and zephyrs sigh,*
> *Where I may come and shed the tear*
> *That streams unbid from sorrowing eye.*

Malinda's headstone was reunited with her body in 1992 and placed in one of the mansion's garden.

The Van Horn Mansion became a museum for the Newfane Historical Society where visitors hear footsteps as well as ghostly conversations and a woman singing. Lights flicker and sometimes even a tall shadow of a man appears. People on the outside looking into the brick building seen to have the most magnificent experiences. Some claim to have seen the face of a woman peering out of an upstairs window. Also, the ghost of a girl, possibly Malina, has been known to run from the property in front of oncoming traffic causing the terrified driver to skid, the apparition disappearing as the car slides through it.

Wayne County Jail

The old Wayne County Jail, which now houses the county museum, was used to confine criminals as well as the residence for the county sheriff from 1856 to 1960. The twenty-four 7'x4'x9' jail cells held infamous local criminals like George DeLue (Boy Desperad0) and big Ed Kelley and his gang, who all came out of the hoosegow alive. For a few, the inside of the Wayne County Jail was the last place they laid their eyes on before they died.

Wayne County Jail in Lyons, NY. It was the site of the only execution in the county.

William Fee, the only man executed in Wayne County, died at 1:30 pm on March 23, 1860. He was sentenced to death by hanging for the September 26, 1859 rape and strangulation of an unidentified woman whose body was found in the brush along Montezuma Turnpike with finger-shaped bruises around her neck. At the time of the murder, Fee was in the Clyde-Savannah area working on the Erie Canal. He and one other man, later identified as Thomas Muldoon, became the prime (and only) suspects in the murder because they had been seen following the woman on the day before her body was discovered. It didn't help their case, that right after her body was found, Fee fled town and later was arrested in New York City. Muldoon was apprehended in Scranton, Pennsylvania. Both men were brought back to Lyons where they were indicted on the charge of murder.

Fee's trial lasted four days with the jury deliberating just three hours. When the guilty verdict was delivered, he was smug with his reply, "Damn tough, but I'm not going to lie awake thinking about it." However, as stalwart as he was, Fee broke down sobbing when the judge sentenced him to death.

Two thousand people gathered, despite a snowstorm, to witness Fee's execution at the jail. The Lyons Life Guards were called to duty to maintain peace and order among the crowd of onlookers. His final words before he dropped to his death, were reportedly the following, "I am not aware of any connection with the death of that woman. I accept death to which I am condemned as an atonement for the sins of my life." After the deed was done, his body was taken to Lockpit, which was where his mother lived. A police officer guarded the grave for a week to ensure that graverobbers did not disturb it. As for Muldoon, he was acquitted of murder by the "death bed" testimony of William Fee. "Fee, after the noose had been adjusted around his neck, begged for a moment in which to speak and took the opportunity to say that he knew no ill of Muldoon (Democrat and Chronicle April 12, 1907)."

Another prisoner that died at the jail was Robert Redder. Redder was unemployed, a husband and the father of seven who loved to drink too much, while his wife practically worked herself to death in order to support the family. Robert continuously verbally abused his wife Ida and on more than one occasion threatened to kill her and himself, most thought it was just the alcohol talking. On July 7, 1903 Redder drank himself into a stupor, got his hands on a revolver and tried to make good on his threats. He confronted Ida with the gun and as she tried to run away, he shot her in the shoulder and hand. Had it not been for two passersby, including an Episcopal minister who tackled Robert, Ida Redder would likely have been killed.

Robert Redder was taken to the Wayne County Jail and was ultimately tried and convicted of attempted murder. The judge sentenced him to seven years at Auburn State Prison, a future that he couldn't stomach. Redder's family and friends refused to visit him at the jail, and he saw seven years of solitude before him. Four days after his sentencing Redder was able to procure some carbolic acid under the guise of needing it to clean an old wound on his leg. He drank the acid and died a horrible death in his cell on October 27, 1903.

The jail is rumored to be haunted by the spirits of former prisoners. Could the strange and disturbing noises be the final agonizing moments of Redder's life playing over and over again? Or perhaps the ghostly manifestations and otherworldly encounters are connected to the gallows and rope used in William Fee's execution. A pair of simple chairs made from the scaffold are housed at the museum. Both the gallows and rope were borrowed from the Monroe County jail and had previously been used to carry out the sentence of Ira Stout in 1858. Fee's execution went off without a hitch, unlike that of Stout.

Just before he arrived in Rochester, Ira Stout had been paroled from Eastern State Penitentiary in Philadelphia after serving a four-and-a-half sentence for armed robbery of a store that he then set on fire. Stout was in love with his own sister who lived in the city and had had a long-term incestuous relationship with her. Sarah was in an abusive marriage with the always drunk Charles Little, whom Ira saw as a roadblock to their happiness together. Ira felt that he needed to free his sister from her hell and the two devised a plan to get rid of Little once and for all. Sarah lured her husband to Falls Field at High Falls a days before Christmas 1857. Ira snuck up behind Little and killed him with a blow to the head with a hammer, he then attempted to throw the body into the Genesee River gorge. But the body landed on a rock ledge just below the bank. Sarah and Ira slipped down the bank when they tried to push Charles' lifeless body over the edge. Ira broke his arm and lost his glasses; Sarah suffered a fractured wrist in the fall.

Unfortunately, it was not in the stars for them to be together. When the body of Charles Little was found the next day, a pair of glasses that were traced back to Ira Stout were found beside it. Both were arrested and convicted of Little's murder. Ira was sentenced to death, while Sarah was to serve seven years at Sing Sing. The execution of Ira Stout was carried out on October 22, 1858 within the walls of the jail. Luckily, it meant that few people witnessed the event because his hanging did not go as planned and things went horribly wrong. When the door dropped and Ira fell through, the noose failed to break his neck. He was slowly strangled before a horrified crowd, his body twitched for nearly seventeen minutes before he finally died. To make sure that he was indeed dead, his body remained hanging for three quarters of an hour. Ironically, before his death, Ira Stout had written in a letter to a local newspaper, "I do not wish to show cowardly tenacity for life, but I consider it my right and duty to live as long as I can."

Wild Man of Steuben County

Bigfoot, sasquatch, wild man or whatever you call the elusive man beast, is part of the animal group referred to as cryptids – which are species that scientists believe to be mythical and unlikely to exist. Native Americans thought different. They called it the Wejuk and believed that the beast resembling the sasquatch lived in the dense forests surrounding their villages. They also believed that some of the creatures were humans with the ability to shapeshift.

The first reported wild man sighting was in 1818 near Sackets Harbor. The Exeter Watchman carried the article on September 22, 1818. *"Sackets Harbor Sept. 6. Reports say that in the vicinity of Ellisburgh, was seen on the 30th ult by a gentleman of unquestionable veracity, an animal resembling the wild man in the woods. It is stated that he came from the woods and then took his flight in a direction which gave a perfect view of him for some time. He is described as bending forward when running – hair and the heel of the foot narrow, spreading at the toes. Hundreds of person have been in pursuit of several days, but nothing further is heard or seen of him. The frequent and positive manner in which this story comes, induces us to believe it. We wish not to impeach the veracity of this highly favorable gentleman – yet, it is proper that such naturally improbable accounts should be established by the mouth, at least two direct eyewitnesses to entitle them to credit.*

The Ellisburgh encounter had only three witnesses, but the sighting of another wild man was seen by a hundred. The wild man was first seen in the Spring of 1869 in the towns of Woodhull and Troupsburg in the foothills of the Allegheny Mountains. The sightings were witnessed over a month's time and terrorized the countryside, striking fear and uneasiness in hearts of women and children, it even had some of the bravest men in the county on edge.

During the four weeks last past a wild man had been prowling around the woods in the towns of Woodhull and Troupsburg, in the southern part of this county, coming frequently into the highways and cleared fields, to the intense terror of women and children, even strongmen...At first, the whole thing was considered by most people to be a hoax, intended merely to frighten old women and children; but as many of the most prominent citizens vouch for the actual existence of the wild man...(Hornersville newspaper).

On June 12, 1869 a group of about 200 men set out to capture the wild man, for no reason than to find out if it was man or beast. The search party was led by Captain JJ Buchanan and began at the home of local farmer SG Brown. After a few hours, the only thing that the hunters uncovered was a campfire and the barefoot tracks of a man in the forest marsh. The men retuned to Mr. Brown's and began to search in the other direction toward the town of Woodhull. About 800 feet from the house, the wild man was spotted. When he saw the men approaching closer, he let out an ungodly shriek and took off through the woods like a scared deer.

A reporter from the Hornersville newspaper was part of the search party and witnessed the wild man himself. Here is an excerpt from the article about what he saw. *"He was barefooted, bareheaded, and wore no clothing, except a pair of soldiers' pants, his hair was black, sprinkled with gray, was from two to three feet long, frizzly, and matted hanging over his neck, face, shoulders, and back, reaching halfway to the ground, his beard reached to the waistband of his pants, and was jet black, this together with the springing jerking hitch in his gait, gave him more the appearance of a wild animal than human being...the wild, glaring bloodshot eyeballs, which seemed bursting from their sockets...For although I have seen the chiefs of 50 different tribes of Rocky Mountain Indians, painted for the war path, and have looked with wonder on the stuffed gorilla, Barnum's 'what-is-it,' and the man monkey, etc., I never beheld anything in the human form one half as hideous as the wild man of the Woodhull Woods."*

The Steuben County wild man was never seen again after the June 1869 hunt. Whoever or whatever it was has never been determined. Similar sightings of beasts in human form have been recorded over the centuries, making New York State fifth in the ranking of Bigfoot and wild man sightings. But are they real? *At some point, a Bigfoot's luck must run out; one out of the thousands must wander onto a freeway and get killed by a car, or get shot by a hunter, or die of natural causes and be discovered by a hiker. Each passing week and month and year and decade that go by without definitive proof of existence of Bigfoot make its existence less and less likely (Benjamin Radford, Skeptical Enquirer, March/April 2002).*

Reigning hide and seek champion!

Witches of New York

Massachusetts is not the only state in the union to hold claim to having witches within its borders. New York has no less than four witch tales. All but one is in Western New York, the fourth is near Saratoga Springs. Although it is slightly out of the coverage area of this book, it is an interesting tale to tell...so I will tell it.

In 1777, eighty-four years after the infamous Salem Witch Trials in Massachusetts, another woman was accused of witchcraft in Salem...Salem, New York in Washington County. The small town as formed in 1764 by a conclave of Scotch-Irish Presbyterians. Reverend Dr. Thomas Clark led a large congregation of the faithful to settle in upstate New York. Interestingly, the town was not named Salem until 1786, after which the witch stories started to fade from memory. After all, two Salems with witches was more than anyone could fathom. It was a very member of Clark's congregation, Margaret Tilford, who was the accused.

When a neighbor and friend of the Tilford's, Archy Livingston had a cow that produced unchurnable cream, he sought the advice of Joel Dibble. It was reputed that Dibble could read the cards, revealing information about anything he was asked. After the cards were shuffled, Dibble told Livingston to cut the deck. The card chosen revealed the answer to his question, what was wrong with his cow. A spell had been cast on the bovine. But that wasn't all that the cards would tell; the identity of the "witch" that cast the spell was also revealed. Dibble told Archy that she was "a short, thick, black-haired woman who had a red-haired daughter." The town was small and there was only one woman who fit the bill – Margaret Tilford.

Livingston when to the magistrate and filed a formal accusation of witchcraft. Tilford was arrested, charges and a trial date set. Why charges were not brought against Joel Dibble is unknown, since reading the cards was also considered a form of black magic. But back to Margaret's situation. From the get-go there was no evidence that she had done anything wrong. While awaiting the trial that could have formerly cleared her, other events overshadowed her case; the country was at war for its independence and the leader of her persecution and very own pastor, Reverend Clark left town and moved to South Carolina. For five years, Margaret and her husband George were targets of hate, gossip and humiliation. When the war ended in 1782 "the subject was prudently dropped," acquitting her of the charge of witchcraft. Although she didn't face the punishment to poor souls endured in 1693, Margaret's reputation suffered irreparable damage. For the rest of her life, neighbors continued to look at her with a suspicious eye until her death in 1807.

The land where Griffis Sculpture Park is near Ashford Hollow in Cattaraugus County was once the prosperous farm of Lewis and Salome Disch. The couple was blessed with a beautiful daughter named Sophia. Sophia would never marry and stayed on the farm to care for her father after Salome passed away. She continued to live as a recluse after both her parents died. She became the subject of rumors, one of which was that she was a witch. All three in the Disch family are buried under a single monument at Rohr Hill near their farm.

According to local lore, the rumors followed Sophia into death. One evening a group of friends were hanging around, when one of the men said he was going to the Disch grave, or the Witch's Grave. His friends told him not to go, but he did not heed their warnings. About an hour later the man returned, but something was wrong. His face was white as a sheet when he showed them his finger, which had turned black at the tip. The story he relayed was an incredulous one. The headstone was covered with moss except for the letter "C" in Disch. He had run his finer along the letter's outline, in doing so it turned his finger black as death.

Kauquatau was said to be a Native American witch laying in the ground of the old Main Street Cemetery in West Seneca, New York on the outskirts of Buffalo. The cemetery was once the land on which her cabin sat. Kauquatau was a healer/medicine woman revered by her people. When the settlers came to the area, they encountered a culture that they did not understand and were afraid of. For this Kauquatau was persecuted as a witch.

The Witch's Walk in Allegany State Park is near Bay State Hill or Ga'Hai Hill, as it is called by the Iroquois tribe. Ga'Hai means witch light, which is appropriate because mysterious balls of light appear on the hill. It is thought, through legends, that the lights were the presence of witches on a different astral plane (from *The Hill of Dead Witches* by Mason Winfield). The area became known as the Witch's Walk due to the supernatural activity associated with the hill, because only witches and wizards were brave enough to travel there. It is also said that if you get close enough to the balls of light, you can see the face of the witch in the glowing orb.

Along with the stories of witches on the hill, there are also tales of a strange creature described as a half man/half deer or the Wendigo. According to Algonquin folklore, the Wendigo was a terrifying beast that had a craving for human flesh.

Youngstown's Ghost

In the late 19th century the village of Youngstown was terrorized by a ghost, according to an 1895 article in the Buffalo Weekly Express. It was, however, not the first ghost to make an appearance where the mighty Niagara River flows into Lake Ontario. A ghost, though people will dispute is not THE ghost, first appeared in the area in 1880. The spirit was believed to be that of a soldier from nearby Fort Niagara who met a violent end. That spirit appeared to his fellow men in uniform sitting, or perched, on top of the flagpole on the parade grounds soon after the man's death. The ghost, or different one, did not show itself to anyone until two years later, and then it was to a man who kept the encounter quiet for nearly a decade. More people came forward telling stories about their encounters with the spirit that apparently shifted into different shapes each time it appeared – manifesting as a humpback whale, a child, a bent old man and even a grizzly bear. The superstitious people of Youngstown saw the ghost as a bad omen, blaming each unfortunate event that happened in town on the spirit, even an earthquake.

www.ingramcontent.com/pod-product-compliance
Lightning Source LLC
Chambersburg PA
CBHW051406290426
44108CB00015B/2181